SOCIAL CONTEXT
and
PROCLAMATION

SOCIAL CONTEXT and PROCLAMATION

A Socio-Cognitive Study in Proclaiming the Gospel Cross-Culturally

---

David Filbeck

William Carey Library

PASADENA, CALIFORNIA 91104

William Carey Library
P.O. Box 40129
Pasadena, CA 91104

Printed in the United States of America

Library of Congress Cataloging in Publication Data

Filbeck, David.
    Social context and proclamation.

    Bibliography: p.
    1. Communication (Theology)   2. Missions.
3. Sociology, Christian.   I. Title
BV4319.F55   1985   266'.001   84-28539
ISBN 0-87808-199-2

---

to
David, Kenneth
Carmen, Catherine

Contents

PART II
The Missionary Faces New Religions
(What Good is Religion, Anyway?)

Figures

Foreword

"Cultural interpretation is the first task of the missionary in communicating the Gospel in a new culture." This is David Filbeck's "main focus."

The title and content of this treatise eventually brought me back to Clifford Geertz's provocative essay, "The Way We Think Now: Towards an Ethnography of Modern Thought" (1982) in which he discusses the transition of an ethnographic concern with cognitive issues from "the cobweb world of mentality" to the "supposedly more tensile one of meaning." (1983, p. 150). The substance of his presentation of this matter nicely sets the stage for Filbeck's timely contribution:

> That *thought* is spectacularly multiple as product and wondrously singular as process has . . . not only come to be a more powerful animating paradox within the social sciences, . . . but the nature of that paradox has more and more come to be regarded as having to do with puzzles of translation, with how meaning in one system of expression is expressed in another— cultural hermeneutics, not conceptive mechanics. In such a form . . . the problem of how a Copernican understands a Ptolemaian, a fifth republic Frenchman an *ancien regime* one, or a poet a painter is seen to be on all fours with the problem of how a Christian understands a Muslim, a European an Asian, an anthropologist an aborigine, or vice versa. We are all natives now, and everybody else not immediately one of us an exotic. What looked once to be a matter of finding out whether savages could distinguish fact from fancy now looks to be a matter of finding out how others, across the sea or down the corridor, organize their significative world (*Ibid.,* p. 151).

To gain valid and validating perspectives on the subject, Filbeck illustrates his exposition of principles with a salutary selection of personal experiences in Thailand, and couches them in citations from, and development of, the theories of an equal variety of social scientists: anthropologists Robert Redfield, A. L. Kroeber, George

Foster, and Eric Wolfe on peasantry; Raymond Firth and Clifford Geertz on culture as a system of symbols, Edward Tylor on animism, and Alan Tippett on the "power encounter;" social psychologists George Herbert Mead, Herbert Blummer and Sheldon Stryker on socialization and symbolic interaction; sociologists C. Wright Mills on the "sociological imagination," Robert K. Merton on attitudes, Alex Inkeles on the "syndrome of modernity" in development, and Dennis Wrong's caution against the "oversocialization" of mankind; and missiologists Peter Beyerhaus on the social context of "pre-evangelism," Donald McGavran on the cultural context of religious conversion; and Eugene Nida on models of cross-cultural communication.

Within such varied theoretical contexts, Filbeck has boldly addressed many controversial issues in his discussions, critiques or evaluations, and in his applications of social science theory to the proclamation of the Christian message. Specialists will perhaps quarrel with the author over certain interpretations of some of these theories, such as his focus upon the social rather than the cultural context, his definition of "development," his characterization of Redfield's usage of the folk-urban continuum as an "evolutionary scheme," whether or not "research in modal personality has been unproductive," or the precision of his chosen model of social anthropology. Others may even fault him for a forgiveable unfamiliarity with specific historical antecedents impinging upon some of his theoretical applications. Nevertheless, his treatment is thought-provoking and enlightening, providing a valuable combination of basic communication theory with a culture-consciousness which will certainly cause the reader to avoid many pitfalls of ethnocentrism and misunderstanding.

I should like to select one of the author's main methodological devises for special comment and commendation. Probably more than the general "model" of social anthropology, Robert Redfield's concept of the folk-urban continuum stands out as the precise framework for Filbeck's principal approach. "The heart of the book," as he points out, is on "preaching the Gospel in different types of societies." The types he selects are Tribal Society, Peasant Society, and Modern Society, with a chapter devoted, respectively, to communicating the Gospel in each. Filbeck's "tribal-modern continuum" is patterned after Redfield's, both initially presented as a typology, as Redfield put it, "to clarify certain problems as to the nature of isolated-homogenous society as compared with mobile-hetergeneous society" (1941, pp. 324-3).

Filbeck, too, is fully aware of the fact that the world cannot be "classified into three discrete types of societies: tribal, peasant, and modern." Nevertheless, he also is aware of the value of the recognition that the isolated-homogenous cultures in one country are more like those in another country, than either of them are like the mobile-heterogeneous cultures in their own countries. Just as Redfield's hypotheses called attention as much to the impact of modernization upon tribal and village life, Filbeck is careful to emphasize "developing society" as of equal importance to that of the three ideal types.

Thus, it is amply manifest that both as "guides to empirical research" (Redfield, *ibid.,* p. 344), and as "reference points" for the study of the constellations of institutions (Filbeck), the continuum is a valuable instrument for study, both as typology for the analysis of societies and as a model of predictable dynamics of socio-cultural change.

My purpose in calling attention to Filbeck's use of Redfield's concept is only partly to commend the application of a model which I have found to possess great heuristic value in teaching over the years. Another purpose is to try to ward off possible criticism by reviewers who may be more aware of many of Redfield's critics than they are of Redfield's own development of these ideas, and who may suggest that Filbeck is putting too much emphasis upon a conceptual model which has fallen into disrepute. It may be shown that the critics in many respects assumed that Redfield dealt in generalized, dogmatic assertion, which only needed the citation of ethnographic exceptions and contradictions to successfully defeat them. Redfield, however, had only offered his ideas on the typology and the continuum in the most tentative and highly qualified fashion, both as to their validity as generalizations from his own data and also their applicability to any other region (1941, Ch. 1 2). He was interested as much in the examination of the processes of secularization, individualization, and social disintegration as he was in the definition of peasantry or "folk" society. He was also as interested in the urban end of the continuum as he was in the more widely discussed "folk" end. Murray Leaf has pointed out that,

> Redfield's framework remained only programmatic, although it was the program most widely followed by anthropologists who were less interested in the reconstruction of "tribal isolates" than in modern complex societies, in both the old and new worlds (1979, p. 267).

Finally, as Edmund Leach has observed, "Unconventional arguments often turn out to be wrong but provided they provoke discussion they may still have lasting value" (1961, p.v.). At worst, by such a criterion, the "folk-urban continuum" is a concept of undoubted lasting value.

Filbeck has also effectively explained "animism" as significantly more than merely a loosely-defined stage of primitive religion or a catch-all for any peoples which do not espouse one of the better-identified religious systems. He has shown its essential relationship to tribal constellations of other cultural institutions so that to characterize a society as "animistic" may have substance and meaning for a widely predictable set of intimately and functionally related cultural values and behavioral features.

In conclusion, Filbeck has written an especially valuable discussion of cultural relativity; has clearly presented the stresses of the bi-cultural identity of the missionary; has elucidated the cultural context of religion—that there is more than merely a set of beliefs and rituals; and has rightly stressed the importance of understanding the process of socialization, i.e., how we/they *got* that way.

This book is at once a study in communications, a study in social organization, a study in contextualization, and a study in cross-cultural methods. The Thai cultural experience puts vivid life into what might have been dry theoretical bones without it.

James O. Buswell III, Ph.D.
The William Carey International University
Pasadena, California, 91104
June 10, 1985

References in the Preface

Geertz, Clifford, 1982, "The Way We Think Now: Toward an Ethnography of Modern Thought," *Bulletin of the American Academy of Arts and Science,* Vol. 35, No. 5, (February). Reprinted in Geertz, Clifford, *Local Knowledge: Further Essays in Interpretive Anthropology.* New York: Basic Books, 1983.

Leach, Edmund R., 1961, *Rethinking Anthropology.* London: Athalone Press

Leaf, Murray J., 1979, *Man, Mind, and Science: A History of Anthropology.* New York: Columbia University Press.

Redfield, Robert, 1941, *The Folk Culture of Yucatan.* Chicago University Press.

Introduction

• "More winnable people live in the world today than ever before. India has far more now than in the days of Carey or Clough. Africa has myriads who can be won. Latin America teems with opportunity. For the Gospel, never before has such a day of opportunity dawned." (Donald McGavran 1970:58-59).

The missionary of today faces unprecedented opportunities in evangelizing the nations of the world. Waldron Scott (1975) predicts that by 2000 A.D. nearly half of Africa's population will be Christian, an increase of 17 percent from the current 33 percent of the population. In Latin America, evangelical Christianity is growing at a rate of 10 percent while the population grows at 3 percent. This same growth rate, moreover, will continue to the end of the century. Even in Asia, where the growth of the church has been the slowest, significant increases in the number of Christians are still forecasted over the next two decades. By the year 2000, Scott predicts, there will probably be more nonwestern Christians in the world than western.

Yet, in spite of unprecedented opportunities for winning the lost to Christ, the missionary also faces many obstacles in fulfilling the Great Commission. He faces the rise of nationalism, and the resurgence of ethnic and tribal loyalties. He must contend with the revival of traditional religion in many places. He must counteract a growing secularization of life which now threatens to engulf the whole world. On top of these developments, people around the world more than ever before are sensitive to "cultural imperialism" and domination imposed on them by outsiders, whether it is in the form of economics, politics or religion.

The missionary from the United States is particularly vulnerable at this point. Many American missionaries, claims Rene Padilla (1975), preach a "cultural Christianity", i.e., they equate Americanism with Christianity to such an extent that they believe people in other cultures must adopt American institutional patterns when they are converted. Dr. Padilla goes on to remark that

> ...in the light of the powerful influence that this type of Christianity has had in what known as the "mission field", the

xv

Gospel that is preached today in the majority of countries of the world bears the marks of the "American Way of Life". It is not surprising that at least in Latin America today the evangelist often has to face innumerable prejudices that reflect the identification of Americanism with the Gospel in the minds of the listeners.

Unparalleled opportunities for the missionary in evangelizing the lost and reaping the harvest! Innumerable prejudices against the missionaries' proclamation of Christianity! What a challenge the missionary of today faces! On the one hand, literally millions of people around the world stand ready to become Christian over the few years because of mission evangelism. At the same time these same people are just as likely to reject Christianity because of the foreign package it comes wrapped in. Yet the challenge must be accepted if the expected harvest is to be reaped.

The challenge that the missionary faces in today's world is nothing less than the challenge of communicating the Gospel across cultural boundaries. The fact that large numbers of people are and will be receptive to the *Gospel* shows how crucial a role *communication* plays in evangelizing the world. Perhaps as in no other time since William Carey began the modern missionary movement is it necessary for missionaries to understand communication and its importance in spreading the Gospel in today's world.

Fortunately, in the past few decades, there have been contributions to the understanding of communication, especially cross-cultural communication, from several fields of enquiry—sociology, anthropology, linguistics, missiology, to name only a few. It is time to bring together these contributions and integrate them into a science which may be applied, on a comparative basis from culture to culture, for the purpose of communicating the Gospel throughout the world. Such an integration is the main orientation of this book. Contributions to an understanding of the world which are diffused and distributed throughout various fields of study, while valuable of and in themselves, are nevertheless valueless for the missionary in the task of communicating the Gospel. Only by correlating these contributions, and systematizing them into an accessible body of knowledge do they become valuable for the cross-cultural evangelist. In the words of the Apostle Paul, it is time to "compel every human thought to surrender in obedience to Christ" (II Cor. 10:5 NEB) for the task of proclaiming the Gospel among the nations of this world.

Chapter 1
An Introduction To Communication

"I don't want to become a Christian," the former Buddhist monk retorted after I had finished speaking, "because when Christians get to heaven they will go hungry." This is a popular folk Buddhist apologetic, used throughout the northern part of Thailand, for not converting to Christianity. This was the first time I had heard the apologetic and my immediate reaction was *Why did he say that?* An answer to this question was imperative, because by not knowing why he believed Christians will starve in heaven it was difficult if not impossible to communicate any further with him the Scriptural reasons why he should still become a Christian and, more importantly, why Christians will not go hungry once in heaven.

The reason for this apologetic, and its popularity, is not found in any book describing the beliefs of Theravada Buddhism, the type of Buddhism practiced in Thailand. The reason is found in the way Thai society is organized to achieve certain religious objectives deemed beneficial to life. Buddhist monks leave their monasteries very early in the morning to collect food for the day. At the same time, faithful lay people stand ready at the side of the road or path where the monks travel in order to donate food. In either case it is viewed as making merit, the accumulation of which is necessary to improve one's personal kharma for future existences. Out of this daily ritual, and in contact with the evangelistic thrust of Christian missions into Thai society, there has evolved an additional reason for making merit in this manner. The food donated to monks gets transferred to heaven to be stored there until the donor arrives after death. A donor may stay in heaven until his store of food is depleted at which time he is born once more into an earthly existence to travel through another cycle on his journey to Nirvana.

Now it is obvious to Buddhists that Christians practice no comparable ritual of collecting and donating food. Consequently, in their view, Christianity is a deficient religion, for while it is capable of being a path to heaven, it makes no provision for the well-being of the person once there. By not providing a ritual on earth whereby a Christian may store up food in heaven, an obvious and uncontested

1

function of religion is missing in Christianity. And since Buddhism provides this function, it is unwise to convert to a religion that doesn't.

BASIS OF COMMUNICATION

Any attempt to communicate the Gospel in response to the above Buddhist apologetic must first take into account at least three factors of Thai society. Two have already been mentioned: the function of Buddhism, especially the ritual of collecting food, and the result of contact with the evangelistic thrust of Christian missions in Thai society. A third factor, which must equally be acknowledged, is the particular segment of Thai society where this belief is held. A missionary in Thailand is likely to encounter this apologetic in rural areas, among people who form a *folk society* (Robert Redfield 1941). The belief that food is transferred to heaven (and a reason why a person should not convert to Christianity) is not normally found among urban people. In urban areas there are more educational opportunities and exposure to the secularizing influence of western contact. Heaven, and other supernatural concepts, are conceived in spiritual or metaphysical terms. But in rural areas, where secularization has yet to penetrate, religious rituals are often viewed as symbols of concrete reality "on the other side".

This concreteness, which stems from the way Thai society is structured, must be built into any response which seeks to communicate further why Christians will not starve in heaven. For a missionary to respond in nonconcrete (metaphysical), perhaps "demythologized", terms, is to speak too much from a western perspective where secularization is the predominate epistemological paradigm in society. Unless concreteness is built into the communication of the Gospel, very little, in the end, will be communicated about heaven in this folk society. Actually, using such an approach to describe heaven and eternal life is not all that foreign to the Scriptures, for the Scriptures describe heaven, including life in heaven, in concrete terms:

> Then he showed me the river of the water of life, bright as crystal, flowing from the throne of God and of the Lamb through the middle of the street of the city; also, on either side of the river, the tree of life, yielding its fruit each month. (Rev. 22:1-2 RSV)

Christians, in other words, have no need to store up food in heaven because food, including water, is already provided. In addition, a tree is planted in the midst of heaven (Rev. 2:7) from which Christians may regularly pick fruit, eat and live forever. Because of such provisions, made possible by God in His role of Father, there is no need for Christians to be reborn and go through numerous cycles of life in order to escape the effects of Kharma.

Let us define communication, whether it is of the Gospel or some other message, intracultural or intercultural, as the above example from Thailand, as the transmission and receiving of a message. (What we mean by message is another matter; our definition is given below.) It is that, but it is also a lot more. At least five steps are necessary in communicating a message.

1) Deciding on what message to transmit.
2) Encoding the message into an appropriate form.
3) Transmitting the form.
4) Decoding, more properly interpreting, the transmission.
5) Receiving the message.

But this is not all in communication. These five steps rest upon a still deeper foundation, a foundation which forms the basis for the transmission and receiving of messages. For a missionary to understand communication, especially cross-cultural communication, he must first understand the basis on which communication takes place. In a real sense, explicating the basis of communication is the main objective of this book, for only when the basis itself is understood can we hope, again in the words of the Apostle Paul, to make the mystery of Christ clear as we ought to speak (Col. 4:4).

What is the foundation on which a message is transmitted and received? More precisely, where does a person begin in communicating with another, and on what basis does the other person receive and interpret the communication? The answer is to be found in the way society, of both the communicator and receiver, is organized. The social organization of the participants, in other words, forms the foundation which underlies communication, the transmission and receiving of messages from one person to another. Consider the response of the former Buddhist monk to my communication of the Gospel. I communicated to him that eternal life in heaven is available through Jesus Christ. He interpreted my message on the basis of what happens in his own society and concluded that since Christianity provides no ritual for donating food, Christians will go hungry in heaven. Only by realizing the particular sociological foundation underlying his response was I able to communicate the Gospel in a way that would answer his objection to becoming a Christian.

The encoding of a message on the part of the communicator proceeds from a sociological foundation; many times, in communication, the foundation also establishes the message to be encoded.

The encoding in turn is received and interpreted by another person on the basis of a sociological foundation. When the respective foundations of the communicator and receiver are similar, successful communication between the two usually results. But when foundations are dissimilar, i.e., when a message is encoded on one basis but interpreted on another, problems in communication arise. These foundational aspects of communication are especially applicable to missionary communication, for it is in this context that a message (in this case the Gospel) is most likely to be encoded on one basis (that of the missionary) but interpreted on another (that of the receiver in another culture). Rarely do people from different cultures share similar social foundations when they communicate with each other.

At this point one may wonder how communication across cultural boundaries can take place at all. Different cultures would indicate that there are different sociological foundations on which communication takes place. Yet people from different cultures do manage to communicate with each other. However, success in cross-cultural communication is attributed more to the similarities found in the human condition (Robert E. Murphy 1979) than in similarities purportedly found among different cultures. For example, people wherever they live must seek food, must clothe and shelter themselves, procreate, fellowship, etc. Since people talk about these basic life needs, regardless of what culture they are in, it turns out that people from different cultures are able to communicate.

Nonetheless, problems persist and misunderstandings occur. These are attributed to the different ways in which the basic needs of life are fulfilled from culture to culture: what a person may eat in one culture may not be available or allowed in another, the person who may become the mate of another in one culture may be forbidden elsewhere, and so on. Where such differences exist, and people from different cultures begin to talk with each other, even their communications about basic life needs will be encoded and interpreted from different assumptions on how these needs may be fulfilled. The upshot is often misunderstanding about what food should be eaten or what is good to eat, about what is modest in dress, what is incest, etc. If misunderstandings may occur over these topics, which form the core of human existence from culture to culture, we can readily see why problems in communication arise when the Gospel is transmitted from one culture to another by a missionary.

DEFINING KEY CONCEPTS

Social organization, the way society is organized, forms the basis underlying cross-cultural communication. This is the working thesis of this book. But as the thesis it also contains several key terms that need defining. What, for example, is social organization? And finally what is meant by society? Since this book is about culture as well, what is culture? And finally what is meant by cross-cultural communication?

To help us answer these questions let us adopt a *model* from the social sciences. A model, as the word implies, is a display or a characterization or what needs to be explained, described or defined. As a device for explanation, a model performs two for us. First it specifies the *structure*, more precisely the structural components, of what is to be described. Second, it presents a statement or claim of how these components function together to form a system. To speak of a sociological model, therefore, entails that society form a system of social relationships. A society is made up of components that interact in various ways.

The model chosen for defining and explaining our key concepts is *social anthropology*. The words *social* and *anthropology* are taken from the two main approaches in the social sciences for the study of man. These two approaches are *sociology* and *anthropology* respectively. While these approaches are similar in many respects, they differ in orientation. Sociology, for example, studies large, complex societies and tends to be more quantitative using formal statistical methods in data collection. Anthropology, on the other hand, studies small-scale societies and tends to be more qualitative, concentrating on in-depth studies to gain an intimate picture of culture (John Friedl 1976). Sociology is usually restricted to a single society eschewing comparisons while anthropology employs the comparative method focusing on all cultures at all times. In social anthropology, however, both orientations are integrated into a single model of social description.

Social anthropology was developed by anthropologists in Great Britain. A.R. Radcliffe-Brown (1881-1955) first combined the sociological approach of the French sociologist, Emile Durkheim (1858-1917), with the anthropological approach of comparing societies and cultures. Bronislaw Malinowski (1884-1942), an anthropologist born in Poland but trained in England, added developments of his own through his several years of research in the South Pacific. An interesting footnote to the early development of social anthropology was the creation of the British colonial empire (Merwyn S. Garbarino 1977). Colonial officials called upon anthropologists for assistence in understanding how tribal societies operate. This led anthropologists to incorporate insights from sociology in their descriptions. This in turn led to an emphasis upon social organization in describing tribal groups.

Social organization is the basic concept in social anthropology, the beginning point in the model for defining both society and culture. There are three dimensions to social organization, a *static* dimension, a *dynamic* dimension and an *environmental* dimension. Let's take a closer look at each of these three dimensions.

The static side of social organization consists of two parts, structural components and function. The first is readily understood but the second, function, requires additional explanation. Function, as used in social anthropology, is a technical term. In speaking of function it is meant that all structural components are interrelated and interdependent, thus forming a *social system*. Being interdependent, each component has a role or function to fulfill in the system. If the role is not fulfilled, then the system breaks down. Consequently, the function of a component in a system is maintenance, more properly its contribution to the total maintenance of the whole system. Conversely, if a structural component fails to be functional in this sense, it becomes dysfunctional causing the social system to break down. In the end, if the component does not fulfill its role, or some other adaptation is not made, the society itself may disintegrate.

Function, also in this sense, becomes a description of the types of interrelationships that exist among the various structural components of a society. Different components interrelate in such a manner, not only to form a social system, but also to maintain a society as a social system. Similarly, when these relationships are skewed the society stands in danger of breaking apart. By describing the functions that structural components fulfill, we in effect are describing how these components relate to each other (including how they become interdependent) in order to form and maintain a social system. What these structural components are, and how they interrelate functionally in society, will be discussed in Chapter II.

There is also a dynamic side to social organization, viz., people who are interacting with the status quo. This interaction sometimes takes the form of *conforming* to the system, at other times *changing* it. Patterns of social conformity and social change, in other words, constitute important aspects in the way a society is organized. What these patterns are, plus the roles they play in communication, will be discussed in subsequent chapters.

Environment, or the ecology of an area, also has an effect on the way a society is organized and how people interact with that organization. An Eskimo society located north of the Arctic circle, for example, will necessarily be organized differently than a tribal society located along the equator in Brazil. Additionally, if the ecology of an area changes as in a prolonged drought or the discovery of an important raw mineral, people may effect changes in the way society is organized in order to survive (in the former case) or take advantage of the discovery (in the latter case). However, while environment is an important dimension in social organization, its relation to communication is perhaps not immediately apparent. This is not to say there is no relation, because there is. If a message, for example, is encoded and later interpreted on the basis of social organization, then environment forms the *ecological context* wherein messages are encoded and interpreted. A person encodes a message as a member of a social group and in a particular environmental setting: similarly, a person interprets the message as a member of a social group and in an environment. Where group membership and environment are the same, communication between two people can be successful. Where they are dissimilar, communication runs a risk of breaking down.

Social organization, as the basic concept in social anthropology, forms the basis for defining society. If social organization is composed of three static, the dynamic and the dimensions—the environmental—then *society is a large group of people internally organized to live in an environment.* Let's look at this definition more closely.

> *... a large group of people. . .* Size is important to a definition of society. For a group of people to qualify as a society there must be a large number in the group.
> *. . . internally organized. . .* A society is formed only when a group of people becomes organized to form various structures performing certain functions for the maintenance of the group; without such internal organization a group remains only a mass of people.
> *. . . to live in an environment. . .* Exploitation of the earth's environment (farming, fishing, mining, manufacturing, etc.) requires cooperation. Since a person cannot survive alone for long, society provides the organizational strategem for cooperating with others.

In social anthropology culture is defined in relation to how society is defined. If society consists of a large group of people organized to live in an environment, then culture may be defined as the *result* of people being organized and living in an environment. Culture is the plan for living (Louis J. Luzbetak 1970) that the group has established for successfully living in an environment. Raymond Firth, a social anthropologist, perhaps states it best:

> If ... society is taken to be an organized set of individuals with a given way of life, culture is that way of life. If society is taken to be an aggregate of social relations, then culture is the content of those relations. Society emphasizes the human component, the

aggregate of people and the relations between them. Culture emphasizes the component of accumulated resources, immaterial as well as material, which the people inherit, employ, add to, and transmit . . . culture is all learned behavior which has been socially acquired (1971:27).

As the product of social organization, moreover, culture plays an important role in communication. If culture consists of all accumulated resources of society that are transmitted and learned, then culture is what is ultimately communicated (Edward T. Hall, Jr. 1973). A message, then consists of a piece of culture encoded for transmission. What is decoded from the transmission is also culture. But more on this in Chapter IV.

With this brief sketch of social anthropology we are now able to define what is meant by cross-cultural communication. Since a message is encoded and interpreted on the basis of the three dimensions of social organization—structure/function, people and environment—the communication of a message becomes cross-cultural when any or any combination of these dimensions, between the sender and receiver, are significantly different. For example, where the number of structural components and their functions differ between sender and receiver, communication between the two becomes cross-cultural, because a message will be encoded on the basis of one set of structural components but interpreted on the basis of another set. This is still true even when the other two dimensions, people and environment, are similar. Communication of a message is also cross-cultural where the structural component and the functions are similar but the people are different, i.e., where they are different racially. Environmental differences, as noted above in the instance of an Eskimo society and a Brazilian tribal society, also make communication cross-cultural.

In the case of the missionary communication of the Gospel, however, not one but usually all three dimensions of social organization are different between the sender (the missionary) and the receiver. The missionary is usually from a western society where there are numerous structural components, the aggregate of which perform complex functions, where the social stock is predominately Caucasian, and where the environment is northern hemisphere and industrial. On the other hand, the receiver of the Gospel message is usually from a society whose structural components are not numerous, nor are their functions complex. The receiver, moreover, is probably of a different racial stock, e.g., African or Asian, and the environment is likely tropical and agricultural. In such a case, if the Gospel is to be truly communicated cross-culturally, the missionary must encode the Gospel message not on the basis of how his own society is organized (complex, Caucasian dominant, industrial) but on the basis of how the receiver's society is organized (less complex, African or Asian, tropical/agricultural). Otherwise the Gospel as communicated will not "cross" from the culture of the missionary to the culture of the receiver, because in the end the receiver will be unable to interpret the Gospel message on the same basis on which it was encoded.

COGNITION AND SOCIAL ORGANIZATION

People form one component, along with structure/function and environment, in the definition of social organization. But people do not, as with other components of social organization, form a passive part in the way society is organized. That people constitute a nonresponsive element in social organization was perhaps more widely held in an earlier, more behavioristic social science. However, this view fell apart under the fact that each society undergoes change and that the one component of social organization largely responsible for change is the individuals who are members of the society. People, in other words, in forming the dynamic element of social organization, interact with one another and with society in general to both maintain and change the way their society is organized.

Characterizing this dynamic element of social organization, therefore, is equally important to the need for characterizing social organization in the previous section. In fact, it perhaps is even more crucial to do so for our purposes; while social organization is the basis for communication, it is individuals (and not social organization) that do the communicating. Consequently, as was needed in the previous section, we need in this section a model for characterizing the nature of this dynamic element, viz., the people who inhabit the social system. There is a second need for such a model. Since individuals not only interact with each other but also with society in general, such a model must also characterize the relationship between social organization, as a totality on the one hand, and people, as but one part of the totality, on the other. Describing the nature of this relationship is one of the major, ongoing concerns in the social sciences. Since the Gospel is proclaimed to individuals living within specific social contexts, understanding the nature of this relationship is equally an important concern for the missionary communicator.

For this model, by which to characterize and understand individuals as members of society, we turn to studies in cognition found in the social sciences. More precisely, since our model of social organization, social anthropology, draws from both anthropology and sociology, we turn to *cognitive anthropology* and *symbolic interactionism* respectively. Both cognitive anthropology and symbolic interactionism, even though from different branches in social science, stress that the meanings given by individuals to objects, events, and relationships in the course of living with one another in an environment are part of the sociocultural scene and must therefore be included in any characterization of social organization. Otherwise a characterization of social organization is incomplete. But while both cognitive anthropology and symbolic interactionism stress meaning, the particular approach that each takes in characterizing meaning is different. Cognitive anthropology (also called ethnosemantics, the new ethnography, etc.), for example,

> consists of a series of principles, approaches, and data-collecting procedures which share the assumption that culture consists of the knowledge one must know or believe in order to behave appropriately in a culture. It has a concern for the categories, plans, rules, and organizing principles of behavior that a person has in his or her mind as a member of culture (Dean E. Arnold 1976).

Symbolic interactionism, on the other hand,

> is a frame of reference or a perspective. It tells the sociologist, for example, that the world as experienced by those persons studied is of critical importance; it suggests that if sociology is to make headway in understanding social order and social change, the sociologist must comprehend the meaning of facts of the environment, of social relationships, and of intra-psychic "forces" as these are provided meaning by the participants in interaction (Sheldon Stryker 1980:8-9).

These socially constructed meanings form a *cognitive map* for individuals as they live together as a group (Phillip E. Hammon et al., 1975). A cognitive map performs two functions for an individual. First, the meanings an individual constructs into a cognitive map from being a member of society, mediate outside stimuli, and influence the types of response(s) he may make toward the stimuli. Second, a cognitive map enables an individual to interpret symbols by which life is organized in society and by which he may communicate to others. In short, a cognitive map forms the link between stimulus and response.

⋅ Mediating stimuli, more properly data, and interpreting the outside world are two basic processes of cognition. But this observation takes us back to an earlier question of this chapter: what is the basis of communication? Only this time the question now asks: what is the basis of mediating and interpreting data? On what basis do individuals form their cognitive 'categories, plans, rules and organizing principles of behavior?' On what basis do individuals interact to construct the symbols necessary for communicating meaning? The answer to these questions, as with the answer to the first, is found in the way society is organized: cognition, i.e., mediating and interpreting data, finds its basis in social organization. It is social organization, in the words of Sheldon Stryker (1980:70-71), that "provides the resources that people use in their interactions with others". Perhaps an illustration at this juncture will help establish the point.

When I moved to live in a small village of the Mal tribe in northern Thailand, my family consisted of two small sons and my wife who at that time was expecting our third child. The Mal practice matrilocal residency in marriage, i.e., where the man goes to live with his wife at her parents' house. This arrangement performs an essential service in Mal society: a daughter, normally the youngest, along with her husband, stay with the parents to take care of them until they die, thus assuring that the elderly in this society are cared for. If a Mal family has only sons and no daughters, as is sometimes the case, the parents face a difficult and uncertain future, for in marriage their sons are expected to move away to live with other families, leaving them with no one to take care of them as a daughter would do. In this case the parents must find for a son a bride who will agree to leave the security of her own family (a security which the tribal matrilocal residency provides for a young bride) and move in with her husband's family. This is no easy task to accomplish.

I did not realize how precarious my future was, in the view of the Mal villagers, until after my third child was born. On returning to the village after the birth, an elderly gentleman came to visit me. He asked what my child was. When I told him the child was a daughter, an expression of relief came over his face. "Now you will have a son-in-law for your old age," he said. Being assured that I would now be spared the agonies of finding a wife for one of my sons, he left. In his interpretation my world was now organized as it should be.

A cognitive map for mediating data also contains assumptions of how the world *should ideally be organized*. Values are also important components to cognition. In Mal society, for example, because daughters are assets to a family in several ways, girls are more highly valued than boys. (As one father told me, a son is fed and clothed for 16 or 17 years and then he goes to work for someone else when he marries.) Every group of people has ideas of the way how their world should be arranged, and how their society should function in a smooth and harmonious way. People also have ideas of why their world is ill-arranged and why there are problems in their society. In tribal or preliterate societies these ideas often take the form of myths or legends which explain the way things have come to be, whether for good or bad. In modern society, these same ideas often take the form of sophisticated sociological and political analyses and solutions; more extreme forms are also found, such as ideology (e.g., Marxism), political radicalism and even cultism.

Our use of cognition in succeeding chapters, however, will not focus on values or ideals. The focus rather will be on the computational processes used in mediating the resources of social organization for the interpretation of messages, especially the Gospel message when communicated by missionaries in other social contexts. Nevertheless, before leaving this section we should touch upon two ramifications that values or ideals, as part of an individual's cognitive map, have for communicating the Gospel cross-culturally.

First, as a communicator of the Gospel, the missionary carries with him a cognitive mapping of the world based on the Scriptures, i.e., a set of assumptions about the nature of the world (its creation and destiny), about man's place in the world ("created a little lower than the angels"), and about the outcome of life (every man shall be judged for the deeds done in the flesh). So often, however, a missionary holds these assumptions implicitly; he assumes that these beliefs are universally held by all people. Consequently when communicating the Gospel in another culture, the missionary does not begin with a description of the Biblical mapping of the world, but proceeds immediately to more advanced doctrines as grace, the plan of salvation, atonement, etc. When this happens the Gospel, especially in a society where Christianity has had little or no impact on the views of the population, is interpreted on the basis of a nonbiblical mapping of the world and in the end may appear incommensurable. If the Gospel is to be properly understood by people having a different mapping of the world, the biblical map of the world must first be explicitly proclaimed.

Second, even though cognition encompasses the ideals and values that are commonly held in a society, it must be recognized that the world as ideally viewed remains ultimately unattainable under present social conditions. It is at this point where the Gospel can be communicated as good news indeed, for through the Good News about Jesus Christ, the Kingdom of God and His righteousness can be established on earth. While Christ's Kingdom is not of this world (John 18:36), the Kingdom nevertheless must not be proclaimed as though it is totally otherwordly and irrelevant to life in this world. The message of the Kingdom, in other words, is still a message for this world, for it is a message of restoration (Acts 3:21), i.e., social renewal for those who believe. Yet, the message of Christ's Kingdom as restoration must not be confused with any particular social order or structure, a confusion that the disciples made after the resurrection (Acts 1:6). The message of God's Kingdom on earth is a message of how a people's mapping of how the world should ideally be organized can truly be realized upon earth. Since cognition is integrally associated with the way society is organized—i.e., how social organization should function for the benefit of the members of society—the Good News about the Kingdom of Heaven is how social organization *through the koinonia of the saints in the church* may now fulfill its intended function.

LANGUAGE, MESSAGES AND SOCIAL ORGANIZATION

A message, in order to be communicated, must first be encoded into a form. It is the form carrying the message that is transmitted, and it is the form that is received and interpreted in order to receive the message. There are many types of form that may be used in transmitting messages. A greeting, for example, may be encoded into a wave of the hand or a toss of the head. Commands to stop and go in traffic may be encoded in a stop light, a four-way stop, or a policeman blowing a whistle and making appropriate gestures. In each case a message is transmitted by the respective form which in turn is interpreted by the receiver.

While there are many forms, language remains the main medium for transmitting messages among members in society. A message is encoded into language, and it is language that is transmitted. Upon receipt, language is interpreted and the message is received.

This process appears clear enough, but it leaves unanswered an important question: *What is a message?* More precisely for our purposes, since language is the principle medium for communicating messages, what is contained in language which in turn is transmitted and received? The answer is found in the way language is structured for transmitting messages.

For our model of how language is structured for transmitting messages we turn to linguistics. Linguistics is divided into two main branches, *formal linguistics* and *sociolinguistics* (Figure 1). The first branch,

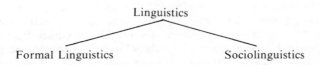

Linguistics

Formal Linguistics　　　　　　　　Sociolinguistics

Figure 1

Formal linguistics, deals with four structural aspects of language: discourse (e.g., conversation, written texts), semantics, grammar and phonology (sounds). The term "formal" is used to characterize these aspects because of certain mathematical-like properties they have in communication, i.e., they are shared by the members of a speech community and may be repeated again and again over the life-span of individual speakers to communicate anything and everything needing discussing. Sociolinguistics deals with two sociological aspects of language. The first, often called macro-sociolinguistics, describes the linguistic divisions of society, e.g., regional dialects, social and class dialects, multilingualism, etc. The second aspect, sometimes called micro-sociolinguistics, describes how language is used in verbal interaction among members of society, viz., *who speaks what to whom when and to what end* (Joshua A. Fishman 1972). Describing the use of language in communication entails descriptions of the communicators (who, whom), situation (when) and goal (to what end).

The two branches of linguistics characterize for us how language is structured for the transmission of messages. A message, in other words, in correspondence to the structure of language, consists of two parts. The first is content, or meaning in its ordinary sense. The second part consists of details of social organizations. Content is transmitted by the categories of formal linguistics while details of social organization are transmitted by the categories of sociolinguistics. Of the two parts, however, the first, content, has received the greater attention since it is perceived to be the more important in communication. This has especially been the case in missions and theology since it is the content of the Gospel—and not its cultural and social context—that is essential for salvation. However, this emphasis on content has led to a neglect of the second type of meaning, details of social organization. This has been an unfortunate neglect, for while details of social organization may not be essential for salvation they are nonethless essential for composing the message of the Gospel so it may be communicated in a social context.

That details of social organization enter and become part of the total message transmitted by language is an aspect of communication that is increasingly being recognized. Social stratification is perhaps the best example of this. Every society is divided into various social classes that in turn are based on the number of statuses and roles available in the society. John Friedl (1976) defines these two terms in the following way. A status is the social position a person holds relative to a particular situation and which is associated with a particular collection of rights and duties. A role is the appropriate and expected behavior attached to a social position in a particular situation.

From this perspective, then, communication begins with one's social status or role in society vis-a-vis the other person(s) one is talking with. Since no two people will have exactly the same set of statuses and roles in society, when two (or more) people are communicating with each other no one person is fully equal with the other as they communicate. The inequalities are based on how society is stratified with regards to available statuses and roles, e.g., a parent speaking to a child, a student to teacher, village headman to villager, and so on. One's status or role in society will often establish what is to be communicated: a parent may order a child to do something while a child may request; a teacher instructs while a student asks for information; a customer asks the price of a product while a shopkeeper seeks to sell for as high a price as possible.

Even when status or role does not dictate the message, communication still does not escape the class structure found in society. The Apostle Paul, for example, when a prisoner and making his defense before Agrippa, addressed Agrippa as one addresses a superior:

> I think myself fortunate that it is before you, King Agrippa, I am to make my defense today against all the accusations of the Jews, because you are especially familiar with all customs and controversies of the Jews; therefore I beg you to listen to me patiently (Acts 26:2-3 RSV).

Paul ended his defense by "testifying both to small and great" how Christ suffered and rose from the dead for "both . . the people (the Jews) and . . . the Gentiles." But Agrippa was fully conscious of his superior social position as he listened to Paul the prisoner, and so sarcastically dismissed Paul's testimony by retorting "In a short time you think to make me a Christian!" Paul did not let this rebuff anger him but continued to address Agrippa as his superior.

> Whether short or long, I would to God that not only you but also all who hear me this day become such as I am—except for these chains (Acts 26:29 RSV).

All languages are equipped to communicate details of social stratification along with content. However, some languages are more equipped to do this than others. Northern Thai, a dialect spoken in the northern area of Thailand, is one such language (David Filbeck 1973). Northern Thai contains more than two dozen pronouns (I, you, he, they, etc.). Their basic dimensions are not gender, person and number as in English, but whether the person one is speaking to or about is superior, equal or inferior to oneself, or whether the person is an intimate friend, an acquaintance or a stranger. Combinations of these social relationships may also occur. In Northern

Thai conversation pronouns are selected and spoken according to the social relationship involved. In this manner significant dimensions of northern Thai social structure become encoded and transmitted by the Northern Thai language.

Various dimensions of social organization become a part of the total message when we communicate by language to others. The ramifications of this fact are far reaching for the cross-cultural communication of the Gospel, especially where the social organization of the communicator (in this case the missionary) is very different from the social organization of the listener. If the social organization of the missionary becomes encoded in the (foreign) language he is speaking as he is communicating, the Gospel becomes "wrapped" in an alien package. As the communication of the Gospel is received and interpreted by the listener in the other culture, the gospel may very well emerge more compatible with the missionary's own social background than with the social context of the listener.

The content of the Gospel—that Christ died for our sins and on the third day was raised according to the Scriptures (1 Cor. 15:3-4)—may very well have been clear enough, but additional and alien features of sociological packaging, which were encoded along with the content in the communication, may cause the total message to be misunderstood as to its applicability for a new social context and therefore be rejected. Indeed, it may be concluded that God has nothing of significance to say in the listener's social environment. For effective communication of the Gospel in another culture, the missionary must make sure that relevant sociological information becomes encoded along with the Gospel, information which will communicate that the Gospel is indeed Good News in society.

PRINCIPLES AND GOALS OF CROSS-CULTURAL COMMUNICATION

Let's review our introduction to communication to this point. How a society is organized forms the basis for communication in that society. Broad organizational patterns found in society form the beginning point for communication. Furthermore, features of social organization become encoded along with content to form messages: communication does not escape the organizational framework of society. Indeed, for a message to be understood in a society, it must be communicated within the organizational framework of that society.

As based upon these observations regarding the relationship between communication and social organization, we are in a position to state the principles for communicating the Gospel cross-culturally.

These principles are: 1) Cultural interpretation is the first task of the missionary in communicating the Gospel in a new culture. 2) The content of the missionary's message remains constant in communication. 3) Communication of the Gospel, therefore, reduces to strategy of communication. Each of these principles merit brief discussion.

Cultural Interpretation. The missionary enters a new culture with a message, the Gospel of Jesus Christ. Two questions immediately present themselves. Will his message be relevant to the new cultural context? If it is not, then how may his message become relevant so it will not be rejected? Without answering these two questions first, the missionary may end up asking and answering questions which do not exist in that culture. To discover how the Gospel is relevant in a new culture, a missionary must first interpret a new culture, i.e., understand the reasons why people do and say certain things. Most people in a culture usually follow the path of least resistance by saying and doing those things which fulfill what is expected of individuals in their culture. Of course, deviance from these expectations occur, but too much deviance on the part of any individual will be corrected, or the individual will be punished. Now what is expected and what is deviant (including how much deviance is tolerated) varies from culture to culture. How a new culture differs in this and other respects must be understood before a missionary can effectively communicate the Gospel in the new culture.

Content of message remains constant. The basic assumption in cross-cultural evangelism is that the Gospel is meant for all; it is indeed relevant regardless of social or cultural context at all times: for "the scripture consigned all things to sign, that what was promised to faith in Jesus Christ might be given to those who believe" (Gal. 3:22 RSV). In our terms, this verse summarizes the *content* of the Gospel message, that part of the message which must be proclaimed in every society. Other aspects of the message, however, namely the sociological aspects, need to be made relevant, or contextualized, for various cultural situations. That is, the Gospel must "speak to" the social context where it is being proclaimed. Contextualization, the Gospel preached and realized in particular socio-cultural contexts, is one of the major issues in missiology today. As a concept it is capable of interpretation and application over a wide spectrum of missiological concerns. On the one hand, the Gospel must take root and grow in specific cultures, i.e., the Gospel (the church, the Bible translated into a new language, etc.) must become recognized as belonging to, or in, the new culture where it is being proclaimed. The Gospel must be "incarnated" in each culture, as God Himself became incarnated through Jesus Christ in a specific sociocultural context, the Jewish society during the time of the Roman Empire. On the other hand, when the concept is applied to the communication of the Gospel, a different picture emerges. At a basic level of meaning, contextualization is the opposite of communication. For in communication there is presupposed a message *transmitted,* while in contextualization there is presupposed a message *created* for the new context. Therefore, the task of the missionary evangelist is communication, and not contextualization, of the content of the Gospel, viz.:

> . . . the great event that took place throughout the land of Israel, beginning in Galilee after John preached his message of baptism. You know about Jesus of Nazareth and how God poured out on Him the Holy Spirit and power. He went everywhere, doing good and healing all who were under the power of the Devil, for God was with Him. We are witnesses of everything that he did in the land of Israel and Jerusalem. . . . (part of Peter's sermon, a Jew, to the Roman, Cornelius, Acts 10:37-39 TEV).

Communication reduces to strategy of communication. This principle follows as a consequence of the first'two principles of cross-cultural communication. If the first task of the missionary is interpreting the cultural context, and the next is communicating the content of the Gospel in a new cultural context, then it falls to the responsibility of the missionary to discover how content (". . . the great event that took place throughout the land of Israel . . .") can best be communicated in the context of a new culture. Indeed, if the term contextualization can be applied to communication, it is only in the sense of strategy, where the "how-to" is contextualized to meet the peculiar demands of a new culture for effective communication of the Gospel.

Of the three principles of cross-cultural communication, the first principle, cultural interpretation, is the main focus of this book. The second principle—content remains constant—is the proper concern of theology and Biblical studies, while the third principle—communication reduces to strategy—is the focus of missiology, or mission as practical ministry. There are two reasons for emphasizing cultural interpretation in the book. First, such an emphasis is in agreement with our desire stated at the outset, of formulating a way of understanding the world; understanding is the result of interpretation. Second, understanding the world is foundational to communicating the Gospel in the world. Just as the Gospel is meant for the whole world, so it is meant for the world in its various cultural manifestations. Just as the Gospel is meant to be proclaimed in the whole world, so it is meant to be proclaimed in the various cultural manifestations of the world.

Even though our main focus is on cultural interpretation, we must recognize that in any proper and complete understanding of communication, all three principles are involved. All three must be integrated in the life and ministry of the missionary as he communicates the Gospel cross-culturally. In other words, before communication has taken place, the missionary must correctly understand the cultural context where he is to proclaim the Gospel, know what the content of the Gospel is, and work out a strategy for making the Gospel intelligible and relevant in the new cultural context. When these three principles proceed in tandem, the Gospel is being communicated.

Integrating these three principles, in the way outlined above, suggests two goals which the missionary must achieve in communicating the Gospel in another culture. They are: 1) communicating the Gospel in a new culture must result in understanding of the message, and 2) the Gospel must be communicated with the aim of persuading people of a new culture to believe and live its message.

Understanding. To the Christians in the northern part of Thailand, the Thai word *khaw cay* "to understand" is nearly synonymous with conversion. After proclaiming the Gospel, for example, in a nonchristian village, and no one accepts their invitation to "enter Christ", the most likely explanation is that the villagers did not understand, implying that if they had understood, they would surely have become Christian. Some people, of course, understand but do not convert; for these people, their failure to convert is attributed to stubbornness, an objecting spouse, kin pressure, perhaps village opposition. All too often, unfortunately, the Gospel as proclaimed by an evangelist in another culture is not understood, or worse, misunderstood. When this happens belief and conversion cannot take place; understanding the Word of God is a prerequisite for conversion, for a person is "born anew . . . through the . . . Word of God . . . the good news which was preached to you" (1 Peter 1:23-25 RSV).

Persuasion. The ultimate goal of any communication is persuasion. And so it must be with communicating the Gospel in another culture and language. "Therefore, knowing the fear of the Lord, we persuade men" (II Cor. 5:11 RSV). Dissemination of information, dialogue, or carrying on a "silent witness" in a community do not qualify as goals in themselves. At best, they are strategies for accomplishing the goal of communicating the Gospel. Whatever a missionary's strategy may be—and there are good and bad strategies—it must be with the aim of converting people to Christ so that God's Kingdom may become established throughout the earth. It is with this final aim in mind that this book is written.

Part I

The Missionary Faces The World
(What Type of World Is It, Anyway?)

Chapter 2
The Sociological Imagination

During the Vietnam War the United States Air Force built several Air bases in Thailand. From these bases USAF fighter-bombers carried out bombing raids over North Vietnam and Laos. But in order to have enough fuel while carrying heavy bomb loads to make their raids and return to base in Thailand, the fighter-bombers had to refuel in mid-air before leaving Thailand's air space. One refueling area was over the small mountain village of the Mal Tribe where I lived. The village was located in the extreme north of Thailand not far from the Laotian border. Nearly every morning for several months in 1965 and 1966 a Boeing K-14 tanker trailed by four Phantom F-4 fighter bombers made several circles over the village on a refueling run. After refueling the Phantoms would break off toward the east and the tanker would head back south. At other times during the day, a low flying reconnaissance plane, on its way into Laos, would sometimes streak overhead leaving in its wake a trail of sonic booms and quivering bamboo houses.

The villagers appeared uninterested in the whole operation, for by this time airplanes were commonplace in Thailand and mid-air refueling, even after describing it and explaining its purpose, was no doubt beyond their comprehension. What really interested them, however, was whether I could build an airplane of the type I was describing, fly one, or both. When I answered I could do neither, the matter was often dropped abruptly and the conversation turned to other topics which made up their world and which they could easily understand.

What type of world was it to these villagers which led them to ask if I could build or fly a modern jet fighter-bomber? How did they perceive the world to be ordered? Because of advanced technology being introduced by Westerners, the vast majority of whom were Caucasians, their view of the world was divided into two parts: their part without technology or at best only a primitive technology, and the other part composing of advanced technologies which were always associated with the white foreigner. This perceived order, moreover, communicated to them that I, as a white Westerner, should be able to construct and pilot a supersonic jet fighter-bomber of the United States Air Force. Their view of how the world was ordered communicated to them information about me, even though it turned out to be false information.

All of us have similar conceptions of how the world is basically organized, e.g., "we vs. they," free vs. communist, white vs. black, savage vs. civilized, developed vs. undeveloped, Jew vs. Gentile, heathen vs. Christian, etc. All such views are valid to a certain degree, some to a greater degree than others. But in being partially valid they are also partially invalid as models for characterizing how the world is organized. Consequently, as with the Mal tribal people of northern Thailand, such views communicate to us inadequate, and ultimately false, information about the world. Our world, in other words, cannot be adequately characterized by simply dividing the peoples of the world into two groups.

The ramifications of this observation are far reaching for the missionary communication of the Gospel throughout the world. If a missionary has only a basic "we-they" view of the world, his view is feeding him false information about how the world is in reality structured, a situation not conducive to the adequate communication of the Gospel in the "other half" of the world. The "they" part of the world is much more complicated and varied than what is normally realized. Unless a missionary understands how varied the world is including the nature of the variations, the only goal he can follow in communicating the Gospel is to remake the "they" into the way he is, for this is the only way he understands the world.

No single person, whether he is a Mal tribal person or an American missionary, can have exhaustive knowledge of the world. No one person can experience all that is possible to experience in the world. This is why each of us have a basic "we-they" view of the world: what we can know and experience of the world belongs to us; but what we cannot know and experience, which is considerable, gets lumped into a single "they" category. The assumption we draw from this inability to know exhaustively the world is that all we do not know is indeed unified. Since this assumption is wrong we need some type of framework which will provide for us a more adequate anlaysis of the world including appropriate classification of the variations revealed by the framework. Only in this way can we formulate the various strategies we need to communicate the Gospel to a complex world.

This is where a sociological perspective comes to our aid, for a sociological perspective provides for us a conception of the world that is more exhaustive and analytical than what our experiences alone can give us. It is a conception that is not dependent upon our internalized "we-they" view of the world, but is a conception which ranges beyond our limited experiences to include the external world as a whole. C. Wright Mills (1916-1962), an American sociologist, termed this perspective the *sociological imagination*. Mills coined this term as a critique of sociology, charging that the difference between effective sociological thought and that which fails rest upon the extent imagination is ultimately used (E.P. Cuzzort and E.W. King 1976). Factual data and statistics in sociological analyses are for the most part meaningless, Mills alleged. What is need "is a quality of mind that will help [us] use [such] information. . . . to achieve lucid summations of what is going on in the world" (C. Wright Mills 1959).

In similar fashion the same charge may be leveled against much of what passes as missionary communication today: where sociological imagination is not employed by the missionary, crucial issues are bypassed and effective communication of the Gospel often fails to ensue.

What is the sociological imagination, or perspective, which Mills urged upon us and which we claim is so important to communicating the Gospel cross-culturally? What is included in sociological imagination? This chapter explores these questions, outlining in essence the broad sociological picture wherein missionaries of today must proclaim the Gospel. As a picture of the world, it will also characterize the sociological basis upon which the Gospel will be received and understood by the peoples of today's world. As we shall see in this chapter, the "they" part of the world is a much more complicated picture than what we normally realize.

THE ORGANIZATION OF INDIVIDUAL SOCIETIES

In the first chapter we saw where a model of social organization must specify first of all the structural components, or building blocks, of society. What are the building blocks of society, out of which social structure is formed? Social anthropology, as our sociological model, specifies that social institutions are the structural components of society. David Dressler and Donald Carns (1969) define a social institution as a comparable durable system of interrelated folkways and laws organized around a given function of society. There are five basic functions in society:

1) Maintaining law and order in society;
2) Producing and distributing goods and services throughout society;
3) Disseminating knowledge and skills to members of society, especially to the oncoming generation;
4) Procreation and nurture of the young including the establishment of kinship obligation and privileges with the view of providing for the aged in society;

5) Providing a rationale for group cohesion including an explanation of one's ultimate destiny as a member of the group.

These functions are realized through the institutional structure of society. Accordingly there are five social institutions: *government, economics, education, family* and *religion*. Every society, whether an isolated tribal society or a modern complex society, has these five social institutions.

Each social institution covers a range of social behavior and belief. While societies will differ according to what area of life is assigned to a particular social institution, every aspect of life is ultimately covered by one or another of the five main institutions in society. To understand an individual society, therefore, and how it is organized, it is necessary to understand, first of all, each social institution and the area of life it includes in that society. Let us briefly survey the basic institutions of society to see what area of life each covers.

GOVERNMENT, as a social institution, has been a favorite topic in social anthropology for quite some time; in fact, it has become a specialty with many social anthropologists under the term, *political anthropology.* Government covers three main aspects of life: form of government, political processes, and law. Every society has some type of formal government; it may be complex as in western society, consisting of multilevel branches of government, bureaucracies, etc., or it may be simple as in small-scale society where government may rest with a leader of the elders. In addition to form there is also a dynamic side to government. That is, a society must be capable of organizing its individual members into action and controlling its members so societal goals can be achieved. Political process, as this dynamic side of government is called, allows a society to mobilize its citizenry, for example, in choosing new leaders, for war, for taxation, and a host of other activities. But along with political process comes a major concern of government in every society. That concern is power, more precisely legitimizing the use of power by certain people in society. Power is a fact of societal life; its use, therefore, must be under proper authority and not misused by unauthorized people for improper ends. The third aspect of government, law, functions in part to define who may use power in society and to what purpose. Law, however, covers a larger area than the legitimization of power. It also includes rules, traditions, and customs which serve to affect and control people's lives. In some societies law is highly codified with its own specialists for enactment, interpretation, and enforcement. In small-scale societies, on the other hand, law is much less codified, consisting mainly of traditions and customs handed down from former generations.

What is the function of government, in all of its aspects, in society? Since function is defined in terms of maintenance, we may rephrase the question to ask: What must government, as a social institution, do so that society may be maintained? M. Fortes and E.E. Evans-Pritchard (1940: xiv) wrote that:

> In studying political organization, we have to deal with the maintenance or establishment of social order, within a territorial framework, by the organized exercise of coercive authority through the use, or the possibility of use, of physical force.

The first task of government in maintaining society, therefore, is territorial security, both from external threat and internal disintegration. David Easton (1959), on the other hand, defines the role of government in maintaining society in more positive terms. Government, Easton states, provides first of all ways and means for members in society to formulate demands, and then to legislate rules for satisfying these demands and finally to administrate what has been legislated. Government must also provide means to adjudicate or settle disputes arising over conflicts in demand formulation, legislation or administration. Lastly, government must provide a means of support, or feedback, for all political processes. Without such feedback from the citizenry a political system cannot long survive.

ECONOMICS, as another social institution in society, is an equally popular topic in social anthropology. Bronislaw Malinowski (1920), for example, observed and described the Kula trading ring among the people of the Trobriand Islands of eastern New Guinea. The Kula consisted of armshells and red shell necklaces which were produced and traded as ceremonial items of great symbolic value. Traders would travel from island to island with these items in hopes of "trading upward" to obtain shells and necklaces of greater prestige. From this initial study of Malinowski's, economic anthropology has been a major interest in social anthropology. It is not an interest, however, restricted to "pure economics," or economics unrelated to other aspects of life. Pure economics seeks to discover the universal patterns of behavior which underlie all economic activity. As such, some economists claim that there is a qualitative difference between, for example, the Kula trading ring of the Trobrianders and the complex monetary economics of the western world. In small-scale societies economics is mixed with nonmonetary aspects of life and so does not necessarily qualify as economics. Moreover, in western society, economics is a major if not the most important social institution in society, whereas in small-scale societies economics plays a lesser role in society.

Economics, however, even if mixed with other nonmonetary

aspects of life, is still economics. Indeed, in economic anthropology, it is assumed that economics interrelates with other aspects of social activity in order to contribute to the maintenance of society. This intereaction, moreover, is found in modern society as well as in small-scale society. Consequently, it is the task of the economic anthropologist to discover how economics interrelate and become interdependent with other social institutions in forming a social system. Specifically, though, economics as a social institution covers seven basic areas of social life: resources (land, raw materials, fishing rights, etc.); investment (e.g., of money and time); labor (exploitation of resources, availability of workers, rights and duties of workers); production (e.g., food, manufactured products); distribution (of goods and products throughout the population); and wealth (e.g., what is profit, its accumulation and use to achieve what types of goals).

How does economics contribute to the maintenance of society? Basically, economics provides the ways and means for individuals in society to gain for themselves the necessities of life: food, clothing and shelter. But man does not live by himself alone. He must cooperate with others in a social setting in order to survive. Economics, therefore, provides for society three essential functions. First, economics establishes socially approved ways of exploiting, through investment and labor, various resources to produce goods and services. Second, economics provides ways of distributing goods and services through marketing in exchange for other goods and services. Lastly, economics, as a social institution, defines certain intangibles such as what ceremonial activity would be associated with production, exchange and consumption of goods. In any society economic activity must often be accompanied by ceremony for legitimation, e.g., a sacrifice to the spirit of a field before cultivation, or an elaborate signing ceremony to formally close a trade agreement between two nations.

EDUCATION is a more recent specialization in the study of social organization. However, certain informal aspects of education have long been a concern of cultural anthropologists. E. Adamson Hoebel (1958:580), for example, wrote that:

> In a tribal group education is life . . . most knowledge comes as a by-product of living, with one or another of the family members as a natural, nonprofessional instructor. And much is learned from play with other children who are just a bit older.

The formal side of education—school, professional teachers, planned curricula, etc., as found in modern societies—was left to sociologists to describe. But it is now recognized that the distinction between formal and informal education (the former belonging to sociology and latter to anthropology) is an inadequate description of what goes on educationally in any society, whether modern or small-scale. Education, it now turns out, is a much more pervasive process in social life, and whether it is conducted in a formal or informal way is only a minor aspect of the whole process. Just how pervasive can be seen when we realize that culture exists not only socially but cognitively as well. That is, all that is culture also exists as knowledge in the minds of the members of a society. "Human knowledge is cultural knowledge" states Judith Friedman Hansen (1979:12).

As a social institution, what are the functions of education in society? Education makes three essential contributions to the maintenance of society. First, education specifies for members of society what is to be selected and considered as knowledge. Given similar ecological surroundings, the external, objective world is much the same for all people; all receive via the senses essentially the same data. Education, therefore, provides for society an epistemological grid for the construction of knowledge out of data so that people can make sense out of the world. Second, education determines how this knowledge is distributed throughout society, i.e., who knows what in society and how may one obtain knowledge which others have. There is a difference, for example, in what women know and in what men know even though both have a lot of knowledge of the world in common. Indeed, culturally there are certain things which either sex would alone know to the exclusion of the other. From this perspective education functions to establish the limits upon the distribution of knowledge in society. Third, education provides for the transmission of knowledge, both from one to another and to the next generation. In this function education provides for society the methods of transmission, what types of knowledge are transmitted by which methods, and who may transmit knowledge in society.

When culture is viewed as human knowledge, we can readily see how crucial a role education plays in maintaining society. Since education as a social institution involves data selection from the external world for the construction of systems of knowledge, each culture then represents a unique selection of data forming a system of knowledge unlike any other system of knowledge in the world. In other words, education functions to give a culture a singular characteristic among all the cultures of the world. This function in turn provides for individual members of a culture a group identity which is distinctive from every other group in the world. More important than the uniqueness of each culture, though, is the transmission of that uniqueness to the next generation, for only when this uniqueness is transmitted to the next generation can it be said that society has been maintained. If education as a social institution fails to provide this function, a society may very well cease to exist.

Our fourth social institution, the **FAMILY,** has similarly been extensively studied in the social sciences. Anthropology, for example, has perhaps focused upon the family more than any other social institution. This is due in great measure to the nature of small-scale, tribal societies which have been the major arena of research and study for anthropologists. In small tribal societies interaction among people is more often than not based on kinship relationship. Kinship, of course, exists because of the prior existence of families, of men and women producing children who in turn must take into account what their biological relatedness means in and for society. Since such relationships are a major part of tribal life, the family has come in for a major share of anthropological research. Sociology has also focused upon the family as a social institution, however from a different perspective. Since kinship ties are greatly weakened in modern society, sociologists have not focused on kinship relationships in their research on the family. Sociologists have focused, rather, on the changing role of the family in society, and describing certain pathologies associated with such changes. One outcome of this emphasis has been recommendations on what type of social services are needed in modern society to maintain strong family ties and to compensate, where such ties are impossible to maintain, for the loss of certain traditional family roles, e.g., Social Security and pension systems, child care programs, foster parents, Medicare, and a host of other programs.

The functions of the family, as a social institution, in maintaining society are obvious. First off, the family has the task of procreation, of providing new members for society. The young, however, need nurturing and molding, so the family has the added responsibility of training the young to become acceptable members of society. But with birth and family there comes kinship relationships, so the family also has the job of defining kinship obligations and privileges for society. Another area of responsibility for the family is care for the elderly. Morever, people die, and because they die, family units disappear, so the family as a social institution must also make provision for forming new conjugal unions among members of society so new members may be born to take the place of those who have died. Marriage, therefore, is a function which the family must provide for, a function which begins again the cycle of birth, nurture, marriage, children, old age and death.

RELIGION, as our final social institution, has perhaps the longest history in the social science field. Both Edward B. Tylor, who wrote the classic *Primitive Culture* in 1871, and J.G. Frazer, who wrote *The*

Golden Bough in 1890, took religion as their frame of reference in describing tribal societies. Their purpose in writing about religion, however, was not to describe the variety of religious beliefs and practices in tribal societies; rather, their purpose was to develop an evolutionary scheme for the origin and development of religion in the world. Tylor, for example, proposed a theory which would unite 'in an unbroken line of mental connexion, the fetish-worship and the civilized Christian.' Many earlier anthropologists thought that the religion of the primitive tribal societies, which had only recently become known to western scholars, represented what man was like in the earliest stages of his religious development. Consequently, by investigating the religion of tribal societies, it was thought we could obtain a glimpse of the religious beliefs and practices of early (in an evolutionary sense) man.

Fortunately, it was not long after the time of Tylor and Frazer that such evolutionary schemes, which sought to connect linearly tribal religion with civilized religion, fell into disrepute in anthropology. This occurred, despite the fact that evolution was growing in popularity in the biological arena, because such schemes were built on an ethnocentric bias which claimed that religion in tribal society was incomplete, inferior, even uncivilized in nature, and that religion in the civilized world, especially Christianity, as then practiced in Europe, was the highest form of religion which had to that time come into existence. Interestingly enough it was social anthropologists who led the way in exposing this ethnocentric bias and expurging evolutionary schemes from anthropological writings on religion in particular and on culture in general (Henry A. Schwarz 1976). E. E. Evans Prichard (1965), for example, laid two criticisms against such schemes. First, they were based on evolutionary assumptions for which no evidence was, or could be, adduced; and, second, they were based on the psychological assumption of the 'if I were a horse' sort. That is, if a horse is lost, all the owner has to do to find it is to first imagine himself as a horse, and using his horse sense (sic). . . ! Such an approach shows nothing about the origin and development of religion. Rather, it shows more about the mind of the theorist than it does about the religious beliefs and practices of early man.

After this, the study of religion took on a more functional approach in the social sciences. When greater in-depth research of religion in tribal society was conducted, it was seen that tribal religion, far from being incomplete, was actually functional in society. In fact, religion in tribal society turned out to be much more the source of social integration and cohesion than religion in western society. This discovery in turn spurred interest in the social functions of religion, both in anthropology and sociology, leading in turn to two basic questions: what are the functions of religion, as a social institution, in society? and, how does religion contribute to the maintenance of society? To answer these two questions is not a matter of briefly summarizing, as we have done for the other social institutions, the area of life covered by religion. Religious content and expression vary from culture to culture too much for any summary to do the subject justice. Furthermore, in our perception of the world, religion is much more at the nexus of communicating the Gospel cross-culturally than the other social institutions. This is why we have devoted all of Part II of this book to a detailed discussion of the functions of religion in society. Nevertheless, regardless of the complexity of religion as a social institution, we can still give a preview of the social functions of religion.

As a social institution, religion performs three major functions. The first function is defining the nature of transcendence. Man is capable of transcending himself and his environment, i.e., he is capable of knowing history, thinking about his destiny, and most important of all, of projecting beyond his temporal life into life after death. Because of such capability, religion defines the meaning of history, what one's destiny is (the goal of history), and, again most important of all, describes the nature of the beyond, or what life will be like after death. In association with this description, religion specifies what it takes, by way of belief and practice, to assure one's destiny and entrance into life after death. As there is an individual side to transcendence, so there is a societal side. The social group also has a history and destiny. Even life after death is not thought of outside the group, socially or congregationally, one belongs to. Consequently, religion performs a second function, viz., defining what the history of the group is, including its historical destiny. In this respect, religion provides the moral basis for society, i.e., the rationale for doing things the way they are done in society. A third function of religion in society is to provide explanations concerning the nature of the world. Man is also capable of reasoning, of posing questions and seeking answers to his questions. Obviously, there are ultimate questions concerning the nature of the world and life which in turn demand ultimate answers. Religion specifies both what questions are ultimate and the answers to such questions.

All five social institutions are interdependent in that each must fulfill its own specific functions in the systems so that the other institutions may in turn fulfill theirs. For instance, if government cannot provide effective social control, or economics is unable to distribute goods and services among all members of a society, then it is difficult for education and the family to fulfill their functions. If religion can no longer provide historical and eschatological certainty for society, then government, education, and family are left direction-less in fulfilling their specific tasks in maintaining society. Such interdependency, or interrelationship, is a part of the way a society is organized, and therefore must also be specified if society is to be described.

At first blush it would appear that all social institutions contribute equally to the maintenance of society. The above brief descriptions of the five main social institutions of society, including their functions, tend to enforce this view. However, it is not necessary that all social institutions carry equal responsibility in maintaining society. It is often the case that they do not. As we shall see below, some social institutions indeed have heavier, or lighter, *functional loads* in main-taining society than other social institutions. In some cases govern-ment, perhaps economics, will carry a heavier functional load in maintaining a society than the family or religion while in other instances family and religion will share the heavier responsibility. Societies will differ according to the functional loads assigned to the various social institutions. The functional load that a social institu-tion carries, whether it is heavy or light or some degree in between, is also a part of the way individual societies are organized. This aspect of function must likewise be specified if an individual society is to be described and understood.

TYPES OF SOCIETIES

The world is made up of individual societies, but not all societies have the same organizational configuration. So a major task in employing sociological imagination to understand the world is to delineate the differences, including the similarities, among societies. The method used in the social sciences to accomplish this compari-son of societies, classifying them into *types*. While the comparative method has become a standard procedure in the social sciences, the ramifications of the procedure has not been fully explored and related to the task of cross cultural communication. As we will see later on in this and subsequent chapters, type of social organization must be taken into account when communicating the Gospel cross-culturally.

For our purposes we shall work with three main societal types: tribal society, peasant society, and modern society. Since each type of society contains the same five basic social institutions, each type is differentiated from the others in terms of functional load and degree of interdependence existing among their social institutions. Let's take a closer look at these three types and see how this differentiation works.

Tribal Society. A tribal society is often described as a *holistic* society. What is meant by holistic? In our terms it means that all social institutions are 1) highly integrated and interrelated, and 2) the functional load of maintaining society is distributed more or less equally throughout all five social institutions. Religion shares an equal load with government, for instance, in keeping society operating. In this respect, the various functions of all social institutions are so interwoven that it becomes difficult if not impossible to isolate them one from another. Each function, at the same time, carries a religious dimension, as well as an educational value, and is a legitimate concern of government, economics and family.

Peasant Society. Robert Redfield (1960) defined a peasant society as a part society. It is a society dependent on an elite or dominating society (a society comparable to modern society; see below). While peasants are self-sufficient (they make a living off the land, they marry, produce and raise children, and they have their own religious tradition and are able to maintain social control among themselves), their society is not. As a society peasants are dependent on the urban elite who are economically and politically more powerful. The elite, moreover, are often bound together by family alliances which have been created through intermarriage among themselves. They also set the standard for religious orthodoxy, including the educational standards for passage from peasant society to membership in elite society. This cleavage affects peasant society in profound ways, most notably in the fact that peasant social institutions are no longer able to function holistically, as in tribal society, but are dependent upon the corresponding social institutions of elite society. In our concept of functional load, peasant social institutions must share part of the load of social maintenance with the social institutions of an elite and dominating society.

Modern Society Modern society is characterized by two main features. First, all social institutions have each become highly "institutionalized", i.e., they are highly visible in society and are largely autonomous in relation to one another. As a result, a modern society contains, among its members, such specialists as politicians, economists, teachers and clergy. Even the family does not escape having its own specialists in marriage counselors, divorce lawyers, child psychologists, and so on. The second feature of modern society is that the two social institutions of government and economics share the heaviest, or most important, functional load in maintaining society with education not far behind. Family and religion, on the other hand, carry by comparison very light loads in social maintenance. Religion, moreover, plays little or no *societal* role in keeping government or the economic system functioning. However, religion may carry heavy functional load on the *individual* level in modern society. In similar ways the family fulfills mainly an affection role for individuals in modern society, leaving the crucial task of socialization largely to other institutions. Yet, in spite of these limited roles for religion and family, modern society keeps on operating. But, by contrast, let the economy fail or the government be undermined by corruption, then there is genuine fear that society may not survive unless reform occurs.

SOCIAL CHANGE

Societies change over time; they do not remain static. Societies change because there is a dynamic dimension to the way a society is organized. That dimension is people, more precisely individuals interacting with each other and with the way society is structured. Individuals are not passive members of society; they do not uncritically and unemotionally accept everything that society and environment offer them. At times individuals will conform to the social system of which they are members; at other times they will choose not to conform. Such deviancy, if it becomes widespread and popular, may affect the way society is organized. In the end, a new social system is created, a system, moreover, to which individuals may once again choose to conform or not.

There are many reasons why societies change. A society may change on its own accord, as for example when the strains of dysfunction become intolerable and the members of a society initiate a change to eliminate the strain, the dysfunctional element, or both. A new invention, or innovative ways of doing things may also cause a society to change. But internal change is perhaps not the leading cause of social change. A society undergoes change more often from external sources. Something new is invented, or some new process is developed, in one society, and while it causes them to also change, it also spreads to other societies causing them to also change (although, it must be added, not necessarily in the same way). *Invention plus diffusion*, therefore, are the major cause of social change today. New technologies are constantly being developed in the modern and industrialized societies from where they quickly diffuse to the rest of the world. In fact, governments from both industrialized and nonindustrialized societies promote the spread and adoption of technology. This diffusion has produced, and continues to produce, profound changes in societies around the world.

Obviously there are many facets to social change in today's world. Even though all aspects are important to understanding social change, we are interested in only one aspect, viz., the effects that diffusion of inventions or new ideas has on the institutional structure of individual societies. The spread of new technologies, for example, from industrialized societies affects the institutional structure of nonindustrialized societies. The result is often that the institutional structure of the latter changes to become more like that of the former.

What is the nature of such structural changes, once they have occurred, in nonindustrialized societies? Remember that each social institution performs a particular set of functions. Now these functions are basic to any society, for they represent basic human and social needs. Theoretically, therefore, it makes no difference which social institution performs what function, or if a function gets shifted to another social institution, for in the end society is still maintained intact. In fact, it is this shifting of function from one social institution to another which we see taking place in nonindustrialized societies as they come under the impact of new technologies.

From this example of what takes place in nonindustrialized societies, we can now characterize what we mean by social change. *Social change is the shifting of functions, which are needed for the maintenance of society, from one social institution to another.* In essence this is what we meant when we introduced earlier the concept of functional load. In holistic societies, we stated, all social institutions carry more or less equal loads in maintaining the social system. In other societies the total load is unequally distributed among the social institutions. In the end, some social institutions carry either a proportionally heavier or lighter load in maintaining society. Such functional shifts can produce extensive social and cultural changes in a society.

One social institution which has felt the effects of such functional shifts in many societies of the world is the family. Earlier we saw where the family performs two essential functions in society. The first is socialization, or raising children to become acceptable members of society; and the second is education, i.e., training children to become productive adults in society. As long as these two functions remain for the family to fulfill, a third function, likewise fulfilled by the family, follows viz., social control. When children are raised to become acceptable and productive adults, society is maintained in an orderly fashion.

But with the introduction of modern technology and industrialization into a society, we see where the family, under its traditional methods of socialization, is incapable of training children to be fully productive. So the government establishes an educational system which takes children at an early age out of the family to train them in the skills necessary for technology. This, in effect, shifts the functions of socialization and education, under the power which the government exercises, away from the family to education, which is now a highly visible and specialized social institution. And since it takes wealth to establish an independent educational system in a society, we see economics assuming a heavy load in the change. When the family no longer provides the predominate model for the socialization of children in society, there is an increase in problems of social control, for under the impact of formal schooling more alternatives for adult behavior are presented to the oncoming generation. These alternatives often clash with the traditional goals of socialization of the family resulting in a lessening of social control over the younger generation. The young accept less and less of the older generation as a model of acceptable adult behavior. To compensate for this, specialized institutions, e.g., a police force, are created in order to assure continuing social control in society.

Religion is another social institution that has felt the impact of recent social changes. Many functions that religion formerly performed for society have now shifted to and become associated with other social institutions. This has occurred, and is currently taking place, in many societies around the world. Earlier we saw that a major function of religion is to define a society's historical destiny. This is essentially a validating function which religion performs for a society. This function gives meaning to history, justification for current conditions, and points forward to certain goals which everyone in society should strive for. Now when religion truly performs this function, there is a religious or sacred quality that pervades society. All of life seems oriented to fulfilling the goals of religion. But under the impact of social change this validating function often is shifted from religion to another social institution. The institution which usually ends up with this function is government. It is no longer religion which validates social action and belief, but it is government, mainly through ideology, which provides the meaning for history and establishes the destiny for society. Government, in this case, becomes a "civil religion", performing many of the functions of religion for society.

It is through such shifting of functions away from religion that a society becomes secular. Notice that in secularization no essential function formerly fulfilled by religion is eliminated from society; these functions are only assigned to other institutions. When this happens, a society loses its aura of being religious. In its place there rises a secular or profane quality which characterizes the society. Life is oriented to the pursuit of secular goals. Explanations about the nature of the world are cast in terms that exclude supernatural causality, or at least are neutral in this regard. Even death does not escape secularization, for whether death leads to life after death is now an unknown. As a consequence, man's capability for transcendence becomes limited to this world alone, perhaps restricted to the arts or to "culture" in an artistic sense.

In social change of the type we have been discussing, it is government, economics, and education that receive the greater functional loads in maintaining society. Social change of this nature is also known as modernization. Secularization and modernization are closely related processes. Secularization is essentially a "desacredization" of certain functions formally thought to be religious in nature, i.e., these functions are shifted away from religion and reassigned to other social institutions. As other institutions pick up these functions, and the process becomes completed, a society is considered modern. Technology, of course, plays a crucial role in both secularization and modernization. It is technology, for instance, that takes the cause of crop failure and sickness, two major religious concerns in tribal societies, from the realm of the sacred and places them under the rational control of man. Governments, in ruling over tribal societies, are eager to promote technology of this type in order to promote the welfare of tribal people as well as to consolidate their power over tribal society. To accomplish these twin objectives, governments initiate modernization programs: funds are allocated, among other things, to select and educate tribal technicians who will be able to implement the new technology in order to improve crop production and the level of health in society. As success comes in these areas of life, as they must under the application of modern technology, a society turns away from being religious to being secular.

THE TRIBAL-MODERN CONTINUUM

The world is made up of individual societies, but not of societies isolated one from another. As social institutions interrelate within a society to form a social system so we may say that individual societies interrelate to form a world system. This is especially true in our modern era. With the rise of mass communication and international travel, the world has grown smaller in a real sense, and societies and nations have become more interdependent, especially for the maintenance of world order. This growing interdependence can be seen in all areas of social life. In economics, for example, one nation provides raw materials and perhaps even labor to another nation which in return produces finished products for consumption. Another example of this interdependency is in education. The western model for formal education—primary school, secondary school, university—is being adopted in societies around the world, thus making these societies dependent on the west for assistance in developing formal educational systems.

While a world government has not emerged despite these developments, international military alliances, peace treaties, trade agreements, etc. still create a certain degree of interdependency in government among nations and societies of the world. Religion also partakes of this international interdependency. Missions from western nations, instead of establishing and working toward the indigenous church in other societies, have created in the mission church a dependency upon the sending church for finances and leadership. Still another effect of this world interdependency can be seen in the family. With the rise of a world economic and educational system, there is a tendency for the extended family (consisting of grandparents, parents, and perhaps married children living in one household) to break up, leaving only the nuclear family (parents and unmarried children) as the main family unit in society.

Because of this interdependency among societies there has developed another phenomenon. The societies of the world can no longer be classified into three discreet types of societies: tribal, peasant, and modern. To be sure, there are tribal, peasant and modern societies in the world, but there are many more which do not fit neatly into this typology. Rather, these societies fall someplace in between the types of tribal and peasant or peasant and modern. In other words, there is a *continuum*, or societal types, from the tribal or holistic society at one end to the modern or compartmentalized society at the other end, with peasant society as a mid-way point between the two.

The continuum was first made a part of the sociological imagination by Robert Redfield (1941). In his anthropological studies in Mexico, Redfield saw that, in place of discreet social boundaries between societal types, there was instead a folk-urban continuum between the tribal villages and the city. Between the two end points there were kinship ties and other communicative links. These served to keep the two interdependent and the continuum functioning. Redfield also discovered that as one moves along the continuum, say, from folk to urban, cultural differences are found at each point. For example, there is a move away from group participation and decision making in societal affairs, as are found in folk societies, and a move toward individualization, as found in urban societies, in conducting one's affairs. Another difference he discovered was a decrease in religious orientation on the societal level with an increase in secularization.

Redfield proposed his folk-urban continuum as an evolutionary scheme describing how and in what stages societies evolve or progress from folk to urban. But as was mentioned above, evolution has not fared too well in social anthropology, and the continuum as an evolutionary scheme has never been widely adopted. For one thing, it is an open question whether change away from folk society toward urban society (or tribal to modern in our terms) represents progressive change or social disintegration. The concept of evolution, especially in its more popular usages, represents only progressive change; but if the change toward modernity is more disintegrative than progressive, then (social) evolution is a myth. For this reason we do not propose that our tribal-peasant-modern continuum is an evolutionary scheme of progressive development. Nevertheless, there is a process discernable, when societies are compared, which begins with conditions as found in tribal society and which moves in terms of social change toward the conditions as found in modern society. Admittedly such a process is discernable more as a general outline of change than in detail as found in any one society. Yet we believe, along with Alex Inkeles and David Smith 1974), that men are not born modern, but are made so by their life experiences. A major task in describing social change, therefore, is explaining the process whereby people move from being traditional to becoming modern.

We propose then that tribal society, as defined and characterized in a previous section, be taken as a reference point for describing and classifying societies. A second reference point is modern society. Between these two reference points, a society may be characterized or classified as being more tribal or modern, depending on the degree of social change, again as defined above, that has taken place. Peasant society, in this continuum, represents a half-way point in terms of social change from tribal to modern society. In other words, our three-way classification of tribal, peasant, and modern now represents a constellation of several social characteristics from which societies may differ in varying degrees.

Figure 2 below displays the tribal-modern continuum as a scale. A society may be classified along a scale leading from tribal through peasant on to modern. Classifying a society in this manner is still based on social institutions and the degree of interdependency they exhibit among themselves in the society, i.e., the functional load each carries in relation to all other social institutions in maintaining society. Since in the continuum we view social change as moving from the holistic nature of tribal society to the compartmentalization of modern society, a society is classified along the scale according to the degree social institutions have become independent of each other, that is to say, how much "institutionalization" of social institutions has occurred in the society. For example, in today's world of the nation-state and the existence of government as a separate, all powerful institution, one of the first institutions to become institutionalized is education. Institutionalization happens when a formal school system is established in a society and specialists are trained to administer and teach in the system. Now a formal school system may be underdeveloped or highly developed depending on how many schools there are, how extensive the curriculum is, how many specialists there are, how many levels of specialization there are, etc. The higher the number in these categories, the higher degree of institutionalization of education there is in society.

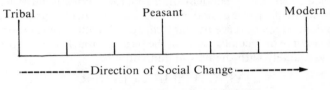

TRIBAL-MODERN CONTINUUM

Figure 2

Religion is another social institution that undergoes institutionalization in the same manner. This is especially true in nations with well developed mission works. Often as a result of mission work religion becomes separated from other institutions of society and its progress is defined in terms of number of church buildings, clergy, adherents, etc. Such quantification, in other words, shows to what degree religion has become institutionalized in society.

To classify a society along a continuum, then, it is necessary to investigate each social institution to discover the degree of independence and institutionalization each has undergone. It may very well be that some institutions have obtained a higher degree of institutionalization in a society than some others. Indeed, this is what we should expect to find in today's world of international aid and modernization programs with their emphasis on political, economic, and educational development. A society may be considered quite developed, for instance, in government, economics or education (i.e., these institutions are independent and highly visible with their own specialists) while still tribal or perhaps peasant in family and religion. Since social conditions cannot remain stable in today's climate of government directed change, a society should be reclassified as conditions change.

A special word about peasant society should be inserted here. Peasant society is more complex than what a construct would suggest. The social institutions of peasant society undergo institutionalization, as our continuum scheme states, but for different reasons. Peasant society is but one part of a greater social system, the other part being an elite society which is in control of the system. This means that peasant social institutions are dependent on the corresponding social institutions of elite society. This development has intensified since World War II. With the independence and creation of many new nation-states, many tribal societies have been brought into a dependent relationship with each other and with central governments. These societies, once holistic in nature and self-sufficient, are now dependent on a separate educational system or government protection, and are tied into a world market system. Such dependencies serve to highlight social institutions, requiring a higher degree of specialization on the part of tribal leaders in order to deal adequately with the new alignment.

TYING IT ALL TOGETHER

We have covered a lot of sociological ground in this chapter. Now it is time to summarize and point out some of the ramifications all of this has for communicating the Gospel cross-culturally. At this time, however, we have space only for pointing out some of the more obvious conclusions and these only briefly. Part II is devoted to spelling out in detail the many ramifications for cross-cultural communication found in using our sociological imagination.

The major theme of this chapter can be summed up in one word: *organization*. This chapter surveyed what should be included in describing how a society is organized: social institution, type of society, social change, and the tribal-modern continuum. The basic component in these is social institution, more properly how social institutions interrelate to form and maintain a social system. By investigating these relationships we are able to define social type, social change, and continuum.

How does all this relate to communicating the Gospel cross-culturally? Consider first a person of a tribal society communicating with a fellow member of his society. The holistic nature of their society (i.e., all social institutions carry equal functional loads in maintaining their society) forms the sociological basis for their communication. Assumptions about the holistic nature of society form the background out of which messages are encoded, transmitted, and interpreted. The same occurs in peasant society and modern society: the nature of peasant society and modern society respectively forms the sociological basis for every communication.

Next consider the western missionary whose social structure involves crucial societal functions for government, economics, and education, but only *individual* functions for religion and family. In communicating the Gospel, for example in a tribal society, conflicts over the relevance of the Gospel for tribal society may ensue unless the missionary takes into account certain broad structural features of tribal society. For as it happens all too often, the missionary's understanding and communication of the Gospel message may be aimed toward the individual while the tribal individual is trying to decide how the Gospel may apply societally. This problem in "cross-societal" communication of the Gospel does not necessarily clear up when the western missionary is addressing a nonchristian from a modern society. Conflict may still arise, for the missionary may believe that his religion and society are integrally related (e.g., Christian Europe, Christian America) while the nonchristian may have a totally secular view of society. Assumptions about the nature of society, in this case, even though both are from similar societal environments do not mesh.

Much more comprise the sociological basis for communication than just societal types, however. Social change, resulting into a continuum of societal types, is likewise a part of social organization and similarly forms crucial elements in the sociological basis of communication. Social change, of course, may result in uneven relationships or functional loads among social institutions. This may create a condition where, at least to the western missionary's viewpoint, certain social institutions (government and education are the more obvious ones) are quite similar to those in the missionary's own society. Unfortunately, when such an observation is made, the missionary may also assume that the other social institutions (e.g., family and religion) are likewise similar to his own society. Hence the Gospel message may be encoded on one basis (because it was assumed that the social institutions in the recipient society are similarly related) but is received and interpreted on another basis (because institutionally all things are not similarly related).

In short, the missionary and the people of the recipient society may be on the same wave length with regards to government and education, and may even be able to discuss these two institutions to the same degree of sophistication, but with respect to religion they may be on different wave lengths. Whatever may be the structural configuration of a society, with regards to social change and its effects, the same will be the sociological base upon which people encode and interpret messages in that society. These differences in the sociological base of communication must be understood and taken into account in the missionary communication of the Gospel.

Chapter 3
The Individual In Society

It is to individuals and not to society that the Gospel is addressed. Consequently it is to individuals we must communicate the Gospel. It is not society we seek to convert, except as a by-product of proclaiming the Gospel to individuals. But while it is to individuals the Gospel is addressed, it is addressed to individuals *in society*. The Gospel is not addressed to the autonomous person divorced from all and every social context. The Gospel speaks to each person in his social environment.

The biblical foundation for these statements is taken from the life and teachings of Jesus Christ. Jesus became a Jew and spoke first of the Good News of the Kingdom to the Jews within their (and His) own context. Then he commissioned the Apostles to spread the Good News to other social contexts by making disciples of the nations. This task, moreover, of proclaiming the Gospel to every person in his own social context was not restricted to the Apostles of the first century, but was given to the whole church throughout all of time to carry out until the end of the ages, so that there may stand before the throne of God "a great multitude—from every nation, from all tribes and peoples and tongues" (Rev. 7:9).

In Chapter 1 society was defined as a large group of people internally organized to live in an environment. Now this definition implies more than just an aggregate of individuals who happen to inhabit a certain environment; it also entails individuals who are recognizably similar in various ways. Similarity in this case does not refer to physical appearance, although dress or costume may be involved. A society is composed of individuals who are similar in views, attitudes, norms, beliefs, in short, people who are similar culturally. How individuals become similar with a social context is a major topic of investigation in the social sciences.

An individual becoming like others in a social context is also a crucial dimension in communication. The reason should not be difficult to see: communication between and among individuals is made possible because of their cultural similarities. To the degree they are similar culturally they will be successful in communicating with each other. This dimension of similarity among individuals in a social context is equally crucial for the communication of the Gospel. The purpose of this chapter is to explore this dimension from the sociological perspective and to discuss the ramifications that this perspective holds for communicating the Gospel cross-culturally. There are ramifications for both the missionary who encodes the Gospel message for communication in a new social context and for the receiver who must interpret what has been encoded in order to receive and understand what the Gospel message is all about.

SOCIALIZATION

A child is born, and in the birth there is once again the potential for uniqueness in a human being. The child in growing up, of course, shall be unique in many ways: his facial lines, the shape and size of his body, and even his voice will distinguish him from all others. Certain mannerisms and styles of speaking may also be uniquely his. In adulthood he may distinguish himself in hunting, laziness, work, art, etc. But even though he may become unique in several ways, there will be many more ways in which the full potential of his uniqueness will not be realized. In fact, if this full potential of his uniqueness, or some degree close to it, were realized it would turn out to be destructive, because to become completely unique in the world is to be unlike anyone else in the world, hence to have no identity, a situation in which any individual would find intolerable if not impossible to survive. To assure identity and survival, then, a child from birth is *reared* to become recognizably similar to others in society.

In being reared the child learns what food is eaten by members of his society, when it is eaten and how it is eaten; what constitutes clothing, how it is put on and when certain types are worn. The child learns to recognize his parents, grandparents, siblings, and what other members of his society are kin and who are not kin. He learns to play, what to worship, whom to hate, how to court, what to do in addressing inferiors, peers and superiors. He learns the proper time, place and manner of relieving himself. As he learns to behave and believe as others in his society, he also comes to expect the same of others. In other words, he learns to predict the behavior of others and if his prediction is not fulfilled he forms a judgment (which he has also learned while growing up) on the behavior, whether it is deviant or still within the range of acceptance. By the time the child is grown he has learned all that is necessary to be counted as a recognizable member of society.

Learning to be a member of society—learning to behave, speak and believe in ways considered similar to others in society—is termed *socialization*. An individual is socialized by means of interacting with others of his society. This particular view of socialization was first proposed by George Herbert Mead (1863-1931). Mead, a social psychologist, was concerned with the question of how an individual developes self-awareness. The answer according to Mead is found not in a psychological investigation of man but in society. An individual becomes aware of himself by first becoming aware that there are other individuals. By interacting with others (e.g., his mother, father, siblings, peers, etc.) an individual next learns to look upon and assess himself in terms of how these others look upon him. In this manner an individual comes to act and behave in ways which not only fulfill the expectations of others but also in ways which are similar to others in his society.

Mead's views regarding the relationship between the individual and society are valuable in helping us understand two important dimensions of socialization, personal identity and the attitudes individuals come to assume as members of society. As we shall see later on in this chapter, an understanding of both is essential for communicating the Gospel cross-culturally.

While each individual is created in the image of God, his identity—i.e., his awareness of who he is—lies elsewhere. A person, for example, is a member of a family, clan, tribe or ethnic group; he comes from a neighborhood, town, province or region and is a citizen of a nation. But identification is not restricted to those obvious categories of reference. A person also gains an identity according to the position or positions he occupies in society. He may, for instance, be poor or affluent, low-class, middle-class or high-class. His identity may be deeply involved in possessions, occupation, education or personal achievements. Furthermore, identity may be multi-dimensional, taking on several of the above aspects to form a composite. Most of all, though, personal identity is associated with the social roles that are available in society.

Common roles found in all societies include mother, father, son, daughter and sibling. As a society becomes more complex and differentiated, more roles become available: e.g., blacksmith, soldier, computer operator, etc. A person, therefore, finds his identity in the role(s) he has assumed. If the number of available roles in society is great, the more complex an individual's identity will be. In our society, for example, a person may be a parent, a professional, a PTA member, a deacon in a church, a shortstop on the church's softball team, secretary of the local Rotary club, chairman of the Boy Scout Committee, and a host of other roles. From this perspective socialization may be viewed as that process which allows individuals to assume those roles that are available to him (or her). Obviously not all roles in society are available, or available on an equal basis to every individual. As a consequence socialization, in addition to preparing people for roles, is also a process by which roles are assigned in individuals. The basis of assignment may be biological (as in motherhood to females and fatherhood to males) or sociological (as when woman's work is in the home and a man's work is outside the home). In either case the role assigned and the identity resulting from the assignment are often considered final and unchangeable.

An individual's attitudes are similarly the product of his social upbringing. Daniel Katz (1960) defines attitude as the predisposition of the individual to evaluate some symbol object or aspect of his world in a favorable or unfavorable light. While man's predisposition to evaluate may be considered, theologically speaking, as the product of creation, the framework for evaluating the external world comes from his social context and is transmitted to him via the socialization process. An important aspect of making an individual a member of society, in other words, is transmitting to him what attitudes he must indeed hold; when an individual comes to exhibit attitudes toward the external world which are similar to those held by other members of his society, he has assumed a significant dimension of being a member of that society.

Growing up to hold socially approved attitudes, however, is more complex than what the preceeding indicates. For one thing, it has long been realized that a person's role, and status, in society will affect the attitudes he has toward the outside world. Robert K. Merton (1964), among his many illustrations of this social fact, reports that commissioned officers generally exhibit a more positive attitude toward the U.S. Army than draftees. Teachers will usually exhibit a positive attitude toward the public school (as offering the education needed for life in our society) than students (who may view school attendance as an intrusian into their lives). On the other hand, teachers may hold some negative attitudes toward the school as a place on employment while administrators, being employers and supervisors, will hold still different attitudes. Examples of this nature from our society can be extended endlessly and can be demonstrated from other societies as well.

Identity and attitude are important dimensions in the socialization process because, when related to available social roles, they add up to personality. Actually personality is much more complex than this; other factors such as emotions and motives are also involved in making up the personality of individuals. But because of its societal orientation sociology has concentrated mainly on the three social components of identity, attitude and social role, in describing personality. A number of social scientists also speak of modal personality types and patterns which most members of society share (Ronald

C. Federica 1970). Unfortunately, research in modal personality has been unproductive because once a basic personality pattern has purportedly been isolated and described for a society by a sociologist or anthropologist, it is difficult if not impossible to find any one individual in the society who fits the description.

This is not to say that the study of personality on the societal or group level is valueless. It means only that we cannot draw reliable conclusions about an individual's personality on the basis of the group he belongs to. On the other hand, we can tie in an individual's personality to the general social scene to observe (1) how his society as a social system sets parameters to the development (in terms of social roles) of his personality (in terms of identity and attitudes), and (2) how he as an individual has adapted to these parameters, i.e., how he has "made his peace" with the "system". Now within the limitations established by society, similarities in personality characteristics will occur from one individual to another, but again the extent of such similarities depends on the two variables of limitation and adaptation on the part of each individual concerned. For example, not every society has an equal number of roles available for its members. A tribal society will not have as many roles available as a peasant or modern society, and while a peasant society will offer more roles to its members than a tribal society it will still fall short of the number of roles available in a modern society.

Since personality and role are closely related, and role and type of society similarly related, we may therefore speak of personality characteristics common to the type of society in question. If, for instance, a tribal person has available only a limited number of roles wherein he can find an identity and on which to base his attitudes, he will exhibit a personality and outlook on life which will fall within the limitations of his (tribal) social environment. The same holds true for the peasant and modern person. Each will exhibit certain personality characteristics (consisting of an identity and attitudes toward the external world) that are in keeping with the roles available to individuals in each society.

A word of caution is needed before leaving this section. In talking about socialization it is easy to draw a picture of man as being oversocialized, i.e., the individual is the victim of his society and has no choice in the matter of what he shall become in growing up. Sociology in its early days was indeed guilty of drawing such a picture of man. But it was Dennis H. Wrong (1961), a sociologist, who exposed the myth of oversocialization. For one thing, Wrong contended, any individual is never completely socialized. If each person were, society itself would never undergo change because each new generation of individuals would be a carbon copy of the former generation. But each person, by interacting with others in his society, grows up acquiring unique attributes as part of his personality. The individual, in Wrong's words, is not completely molded by the particular norms and values of his society. Individuals in being socialized become only similar to and not copies of each other in society.

AGENTS OF SOCIALIZATION

In the previous section socialization was defined as learning to become a member of society. This involves learning how to behave and believe as other members of society. A child learns to become a member by interacting with others in his society. Up to this point, however, the emphasis in socialization has been on the individual learning; even in interacting with others in the focus has been on assimilating what is expected of the individual as he becomes a member of society. There is another side to socialization. As there is the learning side on the part of the individual so there is the teaching side on the part of society. A person does not learn or assimilate something unless it is taught or transmitted to him. Sociologists often term this side of socialization the transmission of culture. Culture, in other words, is the *content* of socialization, or that which is transmitted to the individual so he may become similar to other members of society.

Transmitting culture to a child entails *agents of socialization*. An agent in this case is a fellow human being who has already attained to the status of being a member of society (i.e., who already knows the culture of his society) and who has a stake in socializing the child to similarly become a member of society. In this sense parents and other close kin often become the primary agents in the socialization process. A child first learns, for example, who he is in his family context. Attitudes which the family holds are transmitted to the child. These attitudes may be peculiar to the family or they may be reflective of what is held by society in general. This combination of identity and attitude serves to forge a personality as the child grows to adulthood. Many aspects of this personality may be reflective of this family and upbringing; of course, many other aspects may be reflective of his uniqueness in the world.

Other individuals than family may serve as agents of socialization. Other adults in society also have a stake in the proper socialization of a child. These may be religious specialists, educators, agents of social control such as policemen, employers, and others. Various aspects of society and culture are transmitted to the child by these agents. Peers are also agents of socialization. While a child's peers are not adults, they nevertheless exert a pressure which helps shape the child's identity and attitudes. And as a child and his peers become older and closer to being adults, they assume more of the role of being transmitters of culture to each other. In this regard socialization never stops in life, even though it may slow down in adulthood. As a person goes through various stages of life—marriage, parenthood, middle-age, old age—there are new things to learn and new things to be transmitted.

Interacting—learning and transmitting culture—requires a medium of transmission. Culture may exist, but unless it can be encoded into a medium it cannot be transmitted or communicated to another individual. Herbert Blumer (1937), taking a lead from George Herbert Mead, termed this process *symbolic interactionism*. By this process Mead meant that individuals interact with each other in society by means of symbols. Culture, in other words, first gets encoded into symbols. Next the symbols themselves are transmitted to others who then interpret the symbols in order to obtain the meanings that were encoded.

To Mead, the main medium, or set, or symbols, used in transmission is language. In socialization, therefore, the main medium by which a person learns to become a member of society is language; he learns his identity and what attitudes he is to hold through language. The personality that an individual gains through interacting with others comes through using language. Mead argued that language allows individuals, in growing up, to develop along more complex lines that what behaviorism can account for (E.P. Cuzzort and E.W. King 1976). Behaviorism, as an account of man, is too dependent on discoveries obtained from the behavior of rats and other laboratory animals. Animals, however, interact on the level of signs, but humans interact on the level of symbols. Signs elicit a given response, which is the property of animal behavior, but symbols require interpretation before response can be made. It is this capacity of interpretation which enables an individual to respond to a stimulus in any number of different ways (dependent on the individual's unique set of experiences, mood of the moment, etc.), thus enabling him also to develop beyond more behaviorism as exhibited in animals.

There are other types of symbolism through which individuals interact with others. Ritual and ceremony are two such symbols, body language and gestures are two others. In fact all of culture can be considered a symbolic system to which man responds and through which he interacts with others. (Raymond Firth 1973). Language, of course, remains the primary symbolic system through which interaction takes place. This is obvious, but far from trite, for the task of socialization. Cuzzort and King state that:

If there is a sharing of symbolic content, then interaction is relatively ordered or easy. Where symbolic content is not shared, then interaction is considerably inhibited, although it can continue at "lower" levels. Anyone who has tried to associate with a person who does not speak the same language has found how difficult a social relationship can be. This is an important one because it is so basic and because it is so easy for people to confuse signs and symbols. The use of symbols presumes the existence of a social and cultural system—a network, of values, meanings, interests, concerns, and labelings which are wrapped up in the elaborate form which a language can, in itself, take. (1976:114)

Examples illustrating this dependency upon language before social interaction can take place can readily be found in mission work. Where a missionary does not learn the language of the group among whom he is working, he has little or no social interaction with them. By not learning to interact with members of the group through the language of the group (as any new member born into the group must learn to do), he cannot in reality learn the "network of values, meanings, interests, concerns, and labelings which are wrapped up in the elaborate form" of that language: by not learning their language the missionary cannot communicate the Gospel cross-culturally to members of the group. Of course, interpreters may be used by the missionary, but this cuts off the missionary from the interaction, especially interaction by means of language, with the group. Without this symbolic interaction with the members of the group to whom God has called him, there can be no real communication of the Gospel on the part of the missionary himself.

In interacting through language with the group with whom he is ministering the missionary is in effect undergoing *resocialization*. He is learning to become a member of another society. As with his first socialization, or growing up to be a member of his society, this resocialization will likewise be incomplete; in fact, unless he is an extraordinary individual, he will not achieve the same degree of socialization as he did the first time around. To do so would mean divesting himself of all former identities in order to gain new identities according to available roles in his adopted society, a procedure rarely accomplished by adults. However, to the degree that a missionary can achieve resocialization, learning to become a member of a new society, the better able he will be in communicating cross-culturally. Moreover, as with socialization generally, resocialization is a continued process. A missionary must be ever learning through constant interaction, what one must do to be a member of the society where he ministers. This involves constantly learning new areas of language through which he may interact in every expanding ways with the members of society. He must not leave off learning his new language at the point where he can converse with a few friends, go to the market and preach sermons consisting of the appropriate religious words. Only by expanding his resocialization into every new area of social life will he be able to adequately communicate the Gospel in his new and adopted environment.

SOCIALIZATION AND COGNITIVE STRATEGY

Above we stated that culture constitutes the content of socialization, or that which is transmitted to a new individual to make him a member of society. In Chapter I we stated that culture is also the result of how society is organized in terms of structure and function. Structurally social organization consists of five institutions: government, economics, education, family and religion. Each institution furthermore performs certain functions in maintaining society. Moreover, social institutions interrelate functionally with each other, i.e., each institution carries a particular functional load in relation to all other institutions in the task of maintaining society. Social change, the shift in functional load from one social institution to another in maintaining society, is also a component of social organization. Therefore, what is ultimately transmitted to the individual in the socialization process is the way society is organized for the overall task of maintaining society.

More specifically the particular functional configuration existing among the various social institutions forms the core of what is transmitted in socialization. For example, the social organization of tribal society is holistic in nature; all five social institutions interrelate carrying more or less equal functional loads in maintaining society. It is this interrelated nature of social institutions that is passed on to new generations of individuals in tribal society. The same process occurs for peasant and modern societies, i.e., it is the respective functional configuration existing among social institutions that is transmitted to new generations of individuals in the socialization process.

From the other direction, the individual is learning and assimilating the particular way his society is organized. A person growing up in a tribal society learns that the social institutions, which form the structural components of his society, are interrelated: every aspect of life contains an educational dimension, a religious dimension, and so on. Similarly a person growing up in a peasant society learns that the social institutions of his society are dependent on corresponding institutions in elite society. An individual growing up in a modern society goes through the same learning process except he learns that the various social institutions are autonomous from each other and as a result his society operates often in spite of its compartmentalized nature.

Social change, however, is a trickier dimension in the transmission process than structure and function, because social change has a way of outpacing itself to where the socialization of individuals ends up more incomplete than usual. The older generation cannot transmit all that is or will be necessary for the new generation to know for the future. Hence an individual is unable to learn all that is necessary for life from adults in his society. Consequently, an individual must learn what it takes to be a member of society from agents of socialization other than those who normally act in this capacity. These are agents of change, often educators, government officials or individuals from other societies such as missionaries, who know the direction in which society is changing and can transmit this direction to others. When social change outpaces itself and must be transmitted to an oncoming generation by outsiders, a "generation gap" often emerges between older and younger members of society. This gap may become a serious problem between the generations in a society, or it may be viewed as a breath of fresh air.

Now the functional configuration among social institutions, which also includes the way this configuration is changing in society, establishes for the members of society a cognitive map for understanding the world (Judith Friedman Hansen 1979). As an individual learns the particular cognitive map which his society provides, it in turn becomes a cognitive strategy by which he may interpret and make sense of the world. There are two ways in which a cognitive map functions as a strategy for making sense of the world. First, it functions, i.e., allows the individual, to select data for storage in this knowledge back (E. Thomas and Elizabeth S. Brewster 1976), and, second, to classify data once selected to form systems of knowledge.

The world is full of facts, figures, measurements, events, objects— in short, data. But data of themselves do not form knowledge. For one thing, not every piece of data is considered worth knowing. As a result an individual filters out and selects what should and should not be known. The cognitive map which finds its basis in social organization and which the individual learns through socialization establishes the strategy for selection. Now there can be several cognitive strategies in a society, depending on how complex the society is in terms of available roles and specialization. A tribal society, with few roles available, may offer only two strategies (one for males and one for females) for data selection to its members. A modern society, on the other hand, with its multiplicity of roles, will provide a number of strategies for selecting what should be known and what should not be known.

Of more importance than data selection is classification of data into systems of knowledge. In society the basis of data classification is the social institution, i.e., social institutions are the main mechanism used by individuals to turn data into knowledge. Data have no meaning, or make no sense, unless they are assigned to social institutions, because it is the social institution which relates data to every other piece of data stored in one's knowledge bank. For example, among the Mal of northern Thailand trial marriage is practiced. Trial marriage, of course, is not unknown in America. The Mal, however, assign this custom to the family and consider it an important procedure in assessing the worthiness of a young man to be both a husband and son-in-law. Practicing matrilocal residency in marriage, trial marriage allows the Mal family to test how well the prospective son-in-law will fit in with the family and its work patterns. If he does not fit in, but is lazy, he is told to leave and a new son-in-law is sought. But in America trial marriage is not assigned to the family but, according to the particular segment of society one comes from, may be classified as lust, living in sin, or as a protest to the hypocrisy of conventional mores. In both cases the data (trial marriage) remain the same; only the cognitive strategies for assigning and making sense of the data differ.

In other words, individuals select and classify data, which the world supplies in abundance, according to the social institutions of society and how they interrelate to form social systems. A tribal or holistic society establishes one way of assigning data, a modern or compartmentalized society another way. Since there are several types of societies, or different ways societies may be organized, there are similarly many strategies for data selection and classification.

Social organization provides the cognitive map by which individuals may make sense of the world. But this is only part of the picture. Earlier we saw where man is not totally molded by his social environment, rather he interacts with others thus making his own unique adaptation to the demands of society. In similar fashion as each individual interacts with his own society, so does the individual interact with the particular cognitive map. The result of this interaction is what Judith Friedman Hansen (1979) calls cognitive style. Each individual, in other words, does not accept in toto his society's cognitive map as his own personal strategy for interpreting the world. On the contrary, each individual develops through the socialization process his own cognitive style for selecting and classifying data into systems of knowledge. While numerous cognitive styles may thus develop in a society, the style of any one individual, unless he has grown up deviating in significant ways from society's expectation, will fall within the parameters of the more general cognitive map established by his society. It is the individual's own cognitive style that holds the more interesting ramifications for communicating the Gospel cross-culturally.

COMMUNICATING THE GOSPEL TO THE INDIVIDUAL IN SOCIETY

Even though the Gospel is addressed to individuals, each individual must not be addressed as though he is autonomous. To be sure, evengelism is done on a one-on-one or individual basis, but in communicating the Gospel to an individual one must take into account how an individual has interacted with his social environment before successful evangelism can take place. These social factors about man contain three important ramifications for communicating the Gospel cross culturally.

The first ramification regards the basis on which messages are encoded and interpreted. If a message, as we saw in Chapter I, is encoded and interpreted on the basis of how society is organized, then an individual encodes and interprets messages on the basis of how he has interacted and adapted to that social organization, having become in the process similar (or dissimilar) to others in society. A tribal person, for example, receives and interprets the message of the Gospel on the basis that his society is holistically organized. If the Gospel, as encoded by the missionary, "speaks" to this holism, then the Gospel will be interpreted as relevant. More crucially, though, is the way the tribal individual has interacted with the holistic nature of his society: has he conformed to the demands of a holistic society, or has he refused in one degree or another to be totally in conformity to his society? In either case a tribal person interprets the Gospel message in terms of his conformity or nonconformity to his society. This tension between the demands of society and how an individual interacts with those demands holds true for peasant and modern societies as well. The Gospel is received and interpreted both on the basis of how society is organized and how an individual has interacted with his social organization.

This is equally true for the missionary, who is the encoder of the Gospel message, as it is for the receiver, the interpreter of the Gospel message. Unless he is sociologically and culturally sensitive, a missionary will encode the Gospel on the basis of how his own society is organized and on the basis of how he has interacted with his society. His interaction to the (modern) social organization may be acceptance (as in strict separation of church and state) or it may be reactionary (as in agitating for the restoration of prayer in public schools). Other ways of interaction are also possible. Whatever the case may be, if a missionary, as a communicator of the Gospel, encodes the Gospel message on the way his society is organized and how he has interacted with that organization, then misunderstanding even rejection of the Gospel may very well follow. Since interaction with one's social organization usually produces similarity with others, we may state the problem in another way. If a missionary encodes the Gospel on the basis of his being similar to members of his own society ("To the Jews I became a Jew, in order to win Jews," 1 Cor. 9:20), and not on the basis of similarity with the people of the recipient society ("To those outside the law I became as one outside the law. . . . (to) win those outside the law," 1 Cor. 9:21), misunderstanding and rejection can again occur.

A second ramification for communicating the Gospel cross-culturally arising from man as a social being is in regard to attitude. The attitude(s) a person has toward the missionary and his Gospel message is the first barrier a missionary encounters in communicating the Gospel cross-culturally. Such attitudes may run from hostility to acceptance. As was seen earlier in this chapter, attitudes are transmitted to the individual in the socialization process; when a person has assumed those attitudes toward the outside world which his society wants him to have, he has assimilated an important dimension in becoming a member of society. But the attitudes that any one particular individual may have, in addition to being reflective of his society in general, are also reflective of his particular role(s) in society. Consequently, an individual in a receptor society may in effect be echoing the attitudes that his society has toward the missionary and the Gospel message, or he may be expressing attitudes based on his own interaction with society. In other words, two variables intersect here in the formation of attitudes. One is the social organization and how society has certain "official" attitudes which may be expressed by every member, and the other is the individual's interaction with such official attitudes.

The manner in which these two variables intersect in individuals is important for the communication of the Gospel in other societies. Some societies, for example, are resistant to the Gospel, i.e., they exhibit certain "official" attitudes hostile to the acceptance of the Gospel on the part of individual members. Yet, despite such hostility, it is often possible to find those lone individuals in resistant societies whose attitudes are not so negative to the missionary and his message. Their more positive attitude toward the Gospel may very well be traced back to the way they have interacted with the demands of a resistive society; such an interaction may have established a negative attitude toward his society thus making him more open to new ideas and ways of doing things. Obviously, therefore, in communicating the Gospel in a resistive society, it is possible to win a hearing by seeking out those who, by virtue of their interaction with society, are favorably disposed to the Gospel message.

Naturally in a resistive society there are still those who will be receptive to the Gospel, then in a receptive society there will be those who remain resistant to the Gospel in spite of society's "official" favorable attitude toward the Gospel. Realizing how interaction or experiences can create negative attitudes toward one's own society, a missionary in a receptive society can still find ways to "break through" the negative attitudes (which may be directed more toward society than toward the missionary and his message) of individuals to communicate the Good News of Jesus Christ in a persuasive manner thus bringing them too into the Kingdom.

The third ramification for communicating the Gospel in other cultures emerging from an individual in interaction with his social context is in regards to identity. There are in effect two levels of identity for individuals in society. One is the general identity which society gives, e.g., American, Japanese, Russian, etc. The other is the identity one gains from the role(s) society assigns or makes available to him. To address the Gospel to individuals only on the basis of the more general identity may not in reality be persuasive. In order to communicate so the Gospel message "strikes home", the missionary must speak to the second level of identity, because it is at this level where individuals are more likely to experience the conflicts of life and have fewer answers to the question "who am I?" This is especially true in societies where there are severe role conflicts due to racism, sexism, ideological repression, religious and minority persecution, etc. The roles supplied by society to repressed peoples may be few and/or menial in character and the identities arising from such roles may be resented. Obviously, the Gospel must speak to this type of situation both to the suppressed and suppressor, to bring about reconciliation. Of course, there are societies where no serious conflicts exist between the various roles and identities found among the population. Nevertheless, this happy circumstance does not exempt the missionary, in communicating the Gospel in such societies, from evangelizing individuals in terms of their second level identity.

Identity, as based on social roles, plays an equally important part in the missionary. Since a missionary is assigned roles by *two* societies, his own and the host society, he in effect has two identities. Moreover, there will likely be differences in role assignment between the two societies which in turn may affect the missionary's communication of the Gospel. An example of this effect can be seen when a missionary from a modern industrialized society lives and works in a third world nonindustrialized society. In his home society as a clergy-man his role entails nonpolitical and noneconomical religious activity; in short, exercising essentially a powerless role that is restricted to some vague sense of moral leadership for those who choose to follow him. But as a missionary in a third world society, he may find himself assigned a different role. In this context he may discover that as a religious specialist he has more prestige and influence. He may also discover he has more power than in his own society. However, this may be attributed not so much to his role as religious specialist as to the "economic clout" of his western wealth.

In such a context the missionary gains a new identity, this time based on the power of wealth relative to the economic condition of the host society. Unless he is sensitive to the effects of this wealth in an underdeveloped society, a missionary may unwisely use its power as an additional component in the process of encoding the content of the Gospel into his message for proclamation. That this has occurred all too often can be seen in the paternalistic, even dictatorial, methods that missionaries have used in establishing the church in other societies. Converts to Christianity can be "purchased" either directly or through more subtle displays of wealth and material benefits that wealth brings. If wealth indeed becomes a part of the total message when the Gospel is communicated, it becomes difficult to determine if individuals are converted to the Gospel or to the material benefits that can be gained by attaching themselves to the (affluent) role their society has assigned to the missionary.

There is another aspect to the new identity a missionary may gain in a host society because of his western wealth. His wealth, and the identity gained from it, may lead him to identity with the more affluent in the host society than with the poor. Now the rich must be evangelized as well, and it can only be accomplished by missionaries who have the gift of identifying with them. But this special gift and identification should never be done at the expense of the poor. After all, it is the poor who are the recipients of the Gospel (Mt. 11:5). The missionary must be sensitive regarding this new found identity as based on his western wealth. This does not necessarily mean renouncing his wealth and living on the same economic level as the poor of the host society. It does mean, though, that his wealth must not become a component encoded in his message as he proclaims the Gospel cross-culturally so that individuals both great and small may believe in Jesus Christ on the basis that "though he was rich yet for their sake he became poor, so that by his poverty they might become rich" (II Cor. 8:9).

Chapter 4
Communicating The Gospel In Today's World

Saeng called me aside to ask my advice. His problem was well known through the Northern Thai village where he lived. Being a Christian his problem was also affecting the Church and the application of the Scriptures in a new cultural context.

Saeng and his wife were old and in bad health; Saeng himself was suffering from an advanced case of tuberculosis. Fortunately, they had one asset, an only daughter who had recently married Kuan, a young Christian man from the same village. According to the matrilocal custom of the Northern Thai, Kuan moved to Saeng's house to take up residence as Saeng's son-in-law. Kuan, however, had had enough schooling to realize the health hazard of tuberculosis for the family, and so began to initiate a number of sanitation procedures to lessen the chances of other family members contacting the disease. One practice Kuan recommended was the purchase of separate eating bowls and utensils for Saeng.

Unfortunately, Saeng did not understand Kuan's recommendation; he saw only that he was being cut off from the family communal meals and that in initiating this practice Kuan was usurping his role as head of the household. Consequently, Saeng resorted to what his culture allowed when a son-in-law usurps authority: expel him from the household and look for a new husband for his daughter and a new son-in-law for himself who in turn would show more respect. Saeng demanded that Kuan leave, despite the fact that the family was Christian and the marriage of his daughter to Kuan was a Christian marriage. At this point, though, Saeng ran in to a problem he had not anticipated. His daughter also left, choosing to defy her father and stay married to Kuan. And since Kuan did all the work Saeng was left without anyone to plant rice, take care of the livestock and to do the many other tasks that only a healthy man can perform. Without Kuan he and his wife were condemned to poverty and starvation.

Saeng called me aside to seek my advice on how this problem could be solved. My status as missionary qualified me in his estimation to serve as a counsellor. As I listened I realized any solution would revolve around how Matthew 19:5-6 should be interpreted, and applied, to Saeng's problem:

> For this reason a man shall leave his father and mother and be
> joined to his wife, and the two shall become one flesh. So they
> are no longer two but one flesh, what therefore God has joined
> together, let not man put asunder.

Two alternatives were possible. One was the interpretation which supported the American custom of each couple moving out from underneath parent's authority to set up a separate residence. Under this interpretation there was in reality no problem, because Kuan and his wife had done this; they were now living by themselves in a seperate house. Obviously, though, Saeng had a real problem, and to have dismissed it by appealing to an American interpretation of Matthew 19:5-6 would not have helped him. This left the second alternative, viz., to interpret and apply this verse of Scripture in a way that would be supportive of the matrilocal custom of his society and thus contribute to solving his problem.

To choose the second alternative as a way to help Saeng out of his dilemma, however, required not only an understanding of Scripture but also an understanding (i.e., an interpretation) of the culture of Saeng's society. Northern Thai society, similar to Mal society briefly described in Chapter I, makes provision for its elders through marriage of children and the matrilocal residency custom. The groom moves to live with his bride at her parents' house, and if she is the only or youngest daughter the couple settles permanently with her parents to take care of them until they die. The ultimate function of matrilocal residency in Northern Thai society is to serve as a social security system for people as they grow old. Without children people in this society face hardships and deprivation in their senior years.

Accordingly, I advised Saeng to do two things. One was to forgive Kuan for whatever disrespect he had shown and second to invite *both* Kuan and his wife to return so they could fulfill their obligation of taking care of him according to Northern Thai custom. I assured Saeng that they were a good Christian couple and would do what is right in this matter as the Scriptures command.

> If any one does not provide for his relatives, and especially for
> his own family, he has disowned the faith and is worse than an
> unbeliever (1 Timothy 5:8).

Next I told Saeng that it was against God's will for him to separate his daughter from Kuan. Their marriage vows had been taken before the church and God. No man, even though culture may allow him, had any longer the right to destroy their marriage. Happily, Saeng accepted my advice and invited Kuan and his daughter to return.

They in turn accepted the invitation and returned to resume their duties of taking care of Saeng and his wife.

CULTURAL HERMENEUTICS

In Chapter I we stated that cultural interpretation is the first task of the missionary in communicating the Gospel in a new culture. That is, in order to discover how the Gospel is relevant in a new culture, a missionary must first understand the reasons why people in the receptor society say and do certain things. Without such an understanding, a missionary, in his proclamation of why people should become Christians, may be asking and answering questions which do not exist in that culture.

Why cultural interpretation is necessary should now be clear. *If a person himself receives and interprets the missionary's message on the basis of how his society is organized, then the missionary must have access to that social organization to understand how indeed the Gospel is being interpreted and understood.* If an assessment by the missionary shows that the listener is misunderstanding the message of the Gospel, then the missionary must rethink his strategy of communication to assure that his message will be correctly communicated and understood. Having access to how the listener's society is organized is to engage in cultural interpretation.

Cultural interpretation is currently an important emphasis in the social sciences. The emphasis has focused on either one of two questions, both of which are but two dimensions of a single more comprehensive emphasis: what is the relationship between man and society, and what is the nature of culture. In cultural interpretation man is viewed not as a creature responding to stimuli but as an interpreter of the world around him. The social psychologist, George Herbert Mead, as mentioned in Chapter 3, promoted this view of man through what has since become known as symbolic interactionism, a theory describing how an individual becomes socialized.

But this raises still another question. If man is an interpreter, what does he interpret? The answer is: man interprets symbols. But what are these symbols, or where are they found? They are found in culture; in fact, culture can be viewed as a system of symbols. Individuals growing up in a culture learn to interpret such symbols and use them to communicate with each other. According to Clifford Geertz (1973:52), in his book *The Interpretation of Cultures*, these symbols are "cultural patterns, [those] historically created system of meanings in terms of which we give form, order, point, and direction to our lives." The views of man as interpreter and of culture as a system of (interpreted) symbols, when integrated into a more comprehensive emphasis, form the basis for *cognitive* descriptions of man (e.g., cognitive anthropology, cognitive psychology, etc.). From this perspective cultural interpretation is describing what in society individuals attribute meaning to, i.e., turn into symbols which then become the hermeneutics whereby members of society can understand their world.

The relevance of cognitive and interpretive descriptions of culture for the cross-cultural communication of the Gospel has not gone unnoticed in mission circles. Charles Taber, for example, states that:

> any effort to arrive at a view of the relevance of Scripture to a specific society and culture involves a two-directional task of hermeneutical translation: the human mediator of the message must understand the Scripture itself and translate it into appropriate terms in the receptor culture, and also understand the culture (a hermeneutical task) and translate it back into categories which he can compare with Scripture. (1978)

The relevance of the hermeneutical task in understanding culture, of course, is the main focus of this book. In Chapter I we proposed that social anthropology be our model for understanding how societies are organized. That is, by first analyzing society in terms of structural components and how they function to maintain society, we have the basic categories needed to gain access into the inner workings of culture and thereby make assessments of how the Gospel can best be communicated and understood in another context. To state the proposal in terms perhaps more congenial to the thought patterns of the missionary: social anthropology—with its emphasis on types of societies, social change, social institutions and functions—provides the *hermeneutic* whereby a missionary can interpret another culture.

In other words, cultural interpretation is essentially a *computational* exercise on the part of the interpreter, in this case the missionary. This is in keeping with recent thinking in the cognitive description of man. Jerry A. Fodor (1975:27), for example, states that "the only psychological modes of cognitive processes that seem even remotely plausible represent such processes as computational." Of course, as Fodor goes on to explain, a person must have something through which he can make a computation and thereby come to a knowledge about his outside world. In the case of language and language acquisition, which were Fodor's concern, there must be an innate internal "language" (representation or scheme as it is sometimes called) providing the means whereby a person may make computations and understand what he is hearing.

The same computational process is involved in cultural interpretation. Only in this case the internal language of computation is not innate but learned in the process of growing up to become a member of a society. Nevertheless, once the "language" (i.e., the way one's society is organized) has been learned, it becomes the basis on which computations are made in the interpretation of culture. In adopting social anthropology as our model of social organization, we claim that the components of this form the "language through which a missionary may interpret culture. By computing, for example, what functions are performed by which social institutions, the degree of functional and each social institution carries, and what types of functional shifting have occurred to create various types of societies, a missionary may arrive at an interpretation of the culture of a society. To sum up: social anthropology is a hermeneutic, but to make the hermeneutic work, a missionary must perform various computations.

To do cultural interpretation as a computational exercise, one must work with social variables. Again, in keeping with the choice of our model of social organization, let us adopt the features of social anthropology as the social variables needed for the interpretation of culture. In the case study which opened this chapter, for example, three variables played important roles in understanding what was occurring culturally in Saeng's life: the social institution of family, its function in society, and the type of society in which the case occurred. Computationally, these variables "intersected" to provide an explanation of what Saeng's problem really was and why he felt it was serious: in terms of the social institution, the incident occurred in an extended family consisting of parents, their daughter and son-in-law; in terms of function, the goal of this arrangement in the family was to provide security for the parents; in terms of type of society, the incident occurred in a peasant society in which social welfare for the aged, as provided by government in modern society, was absent. The explanation of the problem was that since the extended family arrangement broke up (when Saeng's daughter left with Kuan) the social function of the arrangement could no longer be fulfilled and, of course, because of the breakup the lack of any other means of taking care of the elderly in this society become grossly conspicuous, especially in Saeng's viewpoint. More importantly, though, having made this interpretation of what was occurring culturally, I was able to communicate what the Scriptures had to say regarding Saeng's problem. The solution to the problem, as deduced from the Scriptures, entailed, in effect, restoring for Saeng the intended function of the extended family structure in Northern Thai society.

The three features of social institution, function and type of society are essential for the computation, interpretation and understanding of culture. But as variables in a schema that may be used in cultural interpretation, one modification must be made. One feature must be taken as the *constant* in the schema while the other two remain as true variables, i.e., features that change values under different conditions. For our purposes here let us adopt social institution as our constant, or the feature that will remain unchanged as we apply the schema for understanding other cultures. The other features, function and type of society, will continue as variables. This choice is not entirely arbitrary. Every society regardless of type contains the five social institutions of government, economics, education, family and religion. Moreover, it is through these social institutions that people in every society organize their lives in relation to each other. On the other hand, not every society is of the same type nor do functions remain associated with the same social institutions across typological boundaries. In fact, it is the shifting of functions from one social institution to another that differentiates one type of society from another.

The best way to illustrate the computational nature of the above is to recast these three features into the form of a *matrix*. Figure 3 below is a Social Matrix for Cultural Interpretation. The symbols F 1 F 2 . . . F n in the matrix represent the various functions that are normally associated with the social institution under consideration.

Social Matrix for Cultural Interpretation

Name of Social Institution⎯⎯⎯⎯⎯⎯⎯⎯⎯⎯⎯⎯⎯⎯⎯⎯⎯⎯⎯⎯⎯⎯⎯

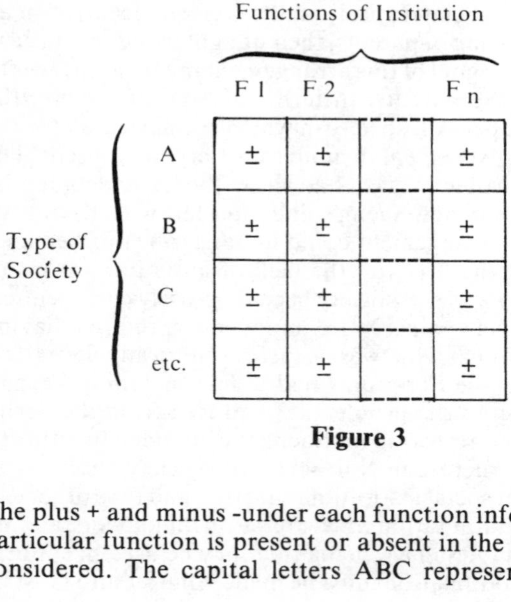

Functions of Institution

Figure 3

The plus + and minus -under each function informs us whether that particular function is present or absent in the type of society being considered. The capital letters ABC represent different types of societies, and depending on one's purpose and classification and number of societal types may be extended beyond the three basic types of tribal, peasant and modern. Furthermore, since a matrix is descriptive of only one social institution, a total of five matrices (one for each of the five main institutions of society) is needed for the interpretation and understanding of culture. (Actually social change in terms of functional shifts from one social institution to another must also be taken into account in cultural interpretation; how this is to be accomplished in the present framework will be discussed below.)

Social matrices, in other words, become devices which a missionary may use for understanding another culture. They may be applied in tandem for a comprehensive view of a culture (e.g., comparing each matrix with all other matrices to see what functions each social institution does or does not fulfill in a society); or individually for specialized purposes. Of the latter application, for instance, a missionary engaged in educational work may focus on what functions are fulfilled or not fulfilled by the social institution of education in his society and thus make an interpretation of the culture relative to his work as an educator. More importantly, after having obtained an understanding of the culture from this perspective, he should be in a better position to communicate the Gospel with respect to the educational aims of the society where he is a missionary. Another example of the use of a social matrix is the study of the economic institution of a society. A missionary, struggling with communicating the concept of self-support to a mission church, would do well to have first an understanding of the functions of economics in the society where the mission church is located. Other examples of using social matrices for cultural interpretation include government (e.g., in understanding leadership patterns for communicating how a church may be self-governing); family (e.g., counseling in times of family crises); and religion (e.g., explaining why Christians will not starve in heaven).

While each of the five major social institutions contain relevant features for understanding culture, we stated in Chapter II that religion is much more at the nexus of communicating the Gospel cross-culturally. Consequently, the social matrix describing religion and its function in society is similarly crucial for the missionary in interpreting and understanding culture. In other words the social matrix for religion is the basic hermeneutical device for the missionary in the important task of cultural interpretation. How the social institution of religion operates in this capacity will be developed in Part II.

THE MISSIONARY AS INTERPRETER

A social matrix is a useful device for the interpretation of culture, but we must not forget that a matrix does not do the "interpreting"; to speak as though it does, as we may do on occasion, is to speak metaphorically. A social matrix for cultural interpretation provides only data arranged in a certain way. While the arrangement may be suggestive or insightful with respect to culture, computation of the arrangement, including whether the data contain insights or not, must be performed by a person. So while a social matrix may contain interesting data, it is still the missionary who must extrapolate meaning from the matrix and make the judgement regarding the value of the data for communicating the Gospel.

The missionary as interpreter is a dimension in cultural interpretation that we must now turn our attention to before we can proceed any further; indeed, to the extent we do not include the missionary dimension in cultural interpretation, to that extent any device for arranging data is meaningless, regardless how interesting the arrangement. The reason why we must now turn our attention to the role of the missionary in cultural interpretation should not be difficult to understand. The missionary is not different from any other person in this regard. He, too, engages in interpreting the world around him, using the same cognitive processes as anyone else. The hermeneutic which he uses to understand the world may be somewhat different than the one used by others in his society, being in his case a combination of how his society is organized and a belief system derived from the Bible regarding the nature of the world and man's place in it.

All this may appear straightforward enough, but a problem may arise when a missionary interprets the type of data that a social matrix provides for a culture other than his own. The problem is this: a missionary may use his own social or cultural background as the basis for the computation and interpretation of a social matrix, or he may override the conclusions to be derived from the matrix and impose an interpretation (as based on how his society is organized) that is incongruent with the matrix. The data and their arrangement in a social matrix may be correct but the actual interpretation of the matrix may be incorrect.

Clearly, assuring correct cultural interpretation on the part of the missionary is crucial for the accurate communication of the Gospel in other cultures. If cross-cultural communication depends on cultural interpretation, then accurate cross-cultural communication depends on correct cultural interpretation. The converse of this also follows: if an incorrect interpretation of a culture is made, then the

Gospel will be inaccurately communicated in that cultural context. Misunderstanding of the intent of the Gospel in and for a new social context will be the result. Persuasion can still occur under such conditions but the resulting conversion may be to something quite different than what was intended.

The problem of incorrect cultural interpretation on the part of the missionary finds its source in the socialization process, i.e., how the missionary became a member of his society. In the socialization process, an important aspect is learning to hold views or interpret data in a manner similar to others in society. When these views or interpretative skills are learned, they "settle" into becoming the hermeneutic for understanding the world. The missionary is subject to this settling process as everyone else in his society, and unless somehow he is made sensitive to what has taken place in his life, he carries the resulting hermeneutic with him into another culture and ends up using it to interpret what is happening there.

Consider for instance the relationship between clothing and Christian morality. In American society displaying certain portions of the human body unclothed in public is interpreted in Christian circles as a symbol of immorality and lust. To state it in our terms: clothing, in the minds of many Christians, functions to maintain society in terms of high moral standards; and displaying the unclothed body in public is dysfunctional, i.e., society is not being maintained but is being corrupted morally. This view is still held by many in American society, even though the consensus is changing regarding how much of the body a person may display in public, uncovered by clothing, and not be considered immoral. Applying this interpretation in other cultures where clothing (or lack of it) and morality are not similarly related, however, establishes a paradigm for communicating the Gospel that in actuality is not relevant for that society. To state it another way: it is now necessary to communicate (as part of the *content* of the Gospel) the message that nonchristians must adopt an adequate amount of clothing to undergo true conversion to faith in Jesus Christ.

Polygamy is another example of the same genre. In America a polygamous marriage is illegal and is viewed in the church as just another symbol of fleshly lust. To rephrase this issue in our terms: monogamy functions to maintain American society in terms of the sanctity of marriage and stability of the family. Polygamy, it is believed, achieves just the opposite. Having more than one spouse does not make marriage holy, thus creating unbearable strains on the family. Furthermore, since in American society adultery achieves the same results, polygamy and adultery become associated in many Christians' minds. Consequently, as has happened in many missionary situations, on confronting polygamy the missionary interprets the practice in terms of lust or adultery, not in terms of what may be the function of polygamy in that society. As with the issue of clothing and morality, a new paradigm for communicating the Gospel is thus established. This time, as part of the content of the Gospel, a nonchristian who has married several wives must do away with all but one to demonstrate he has turned from the practice of fleshly lust to faith in Jesus Christ.

How may the missionary communicator solve the problem of incorrect cultural interpretation? How may the missionary transcend his own socialization in order to make correct interpretations of other cultures? The problem is not a new one, nor is it restricted to missionaries. The problem has also plagued sociologists and anthropologists. However, a solution for solving this problem has been formulated in the social sciences: it is called *cultural relativity*.

Various definitions of cultural relativity have been given in the social sciences. It essentially means that the culture of a society has an integrity of its own and is not intrinsically inferior or superior to any other culture. In our terms cultural integrity means that the components of social organization are functional and generally meet the needs of society's members. The social institutions interrelate to form a social system. It is this system that has an internal consistency or "truth" of its own and therefore should be respected by the outsider for its own sake. An outsider should not be so ethnocentric as to believe that his own culture is superior to other cultures. Most problems of incorrect cultural interpretation, on the part of missionaries and others, stem from ethnocentrism, a lack of respect for the internal consistency that other cultures may exhibit.

Cultural relativity has not been well received in theology. The reason stems from differing concepts of truth in theology and the social sciences. In theology, truth is viewed primarily as consisting of propositions; therefore, what is true propositionally in one cultural context is truth in another. In cultural relativity, however, truth is *systematic*, i.e., truth is in relation to a system. When applied to social systems this means that truth is relative to the social system; what is true propositionally in one cultural context may or may not be true in another. Obviously, this latter view of truth is upsetting to those who hold that revelation consists of propositions that, if the Great Commission is to be fulfilled, must be proclaimed as such in every cultural context. Even more upsetting are the ramifications with regard to the more general questions of what is truth and how we can know truth. If truth, even as propositions, is relative to the context, it can be argued, one context can cancel out another; hence, truth is placed in the role of canceling out itself. As a result, we end up at best of not knowing what is truth or at worse with nothing being truth. Therefore, to carry the argument further, to speak about truth is nonsensical, if not irrational. Small wonder, then, why theologians grounded in the propositions of the Scriptures are troubled by this view of truth and why a missionary may be reluctant to entertain interpretations of cultural data other than those based on his own culture on entering a new social context. To do so would appear to cancel out the truth of the Scriptures for his (the missionary's) own home social context.

The issues at this point arising from cultural relativity are, I believe, overstated. There are three reasons for this assessment. For one thing, cultural relativity does not deny propositions or even absolutes—certainly technology requires operational absolutes that hold true regardless of social or cultural context (cf. Robert Redfield 1953). What is required is that the *basis* for such propositions and absolutes be found outside of culture. For technology the basis is found in physics and mathematics. For the propositions or absolutes of theology the basis is found in Biblical revelation. Second, while cultural relativity does not deny propositions, it does require that propositions (and absolutes) be *relatable* to a system in order to be true with in the system. A proposition may be an absolute, but if it cannot be related to another social system, it cannot be said to be true for that social system. Only by showing how it is related to the culture of the new social system may we say that the proposition is also true for the social system in question. The operational absolutes of technology, for example, in order to be true in a given social system, must be relatable to the functions (food production, transportation, political processes, etc.) of the new content. If they cannot be related—or worse yet they prove disruptive!—then we must say they are not truth for that social system, even though they are still true technologically. Third, the real issue regarding truth does not stem from cultural relativity but from *naturalism*. Naturalism is a philosophical position requiring that explanations for events and relationships in this world be found naturally without recourse to supernatural intervention. Now naturalism happens to use cultural relativity as a stategem in its natural explanation of today's world. Cultural relativity itself makes no demands one way or the other regarding the existence or nonexistence of God, or whether God has revealed certain absolutes for communication in every cultural context; only naturalism makes such requirements.

Blaine E. Mercer and Jules J. Wanderer (1970) define cultural relativity as "judging a person in terms of the culture available to him." This particular definition contains several ramifications highly appropriate for our purposes. First, it admits judging (an interpretive act) and, second, it specifies the standard or "truth", culture in this case, upon which judgment is based. Yet, it is not any culture that may become the standard; only that which is available to the person may be the legitimate standard judgment. It is illegitimate to adopt the norms and values of an alien culture as the criteria for judging a person. Judging is possible, even necessary as an act of being human, but it should be done only within the cultural context of the person being judged.

The above definition and discussion of cultural relativity leads, I believe, to what the Apostle Paul was saying in Romans 2:14-16.

> The Gentiles do not have the Law; but whenever of their free will they do what the Law commands, they are a law to themselves, even though they do not have the Law. Their conduct shows that what the Law commands is written in their hearts. Their consciences also show that this is true, since their thoughts sometimes accuse them and sometimes defend them. And so, according to the Good News I preach, this is how it will be on that Day when God, through Jesus Christ, will judge the secret thoughts of men (NEV).

God will judge nonchristians according to what has been available to them, viz., the law written in their hearts (= the norms and values of their culture where these compare to what God revealed through the cultural context of the Israelites), and how conscientiously they have followed this law. Moreover, nonchristians have a real knowledge of what is right and wrong (i.e., knowledge whose truth is relative to the culture involved) and it is this knowledge that accuses or defends them.

A further word of exposition is perhaps needed here. Far from supporting the possibility of salvation by means of culture, good morals or a clear conscience apart from Jesus Christ, this interpretation of Romans 2:14-16 necessitates the doctrine of salvation by faith in Jesus Christ alone. As Paul develops the argument in the succeeding chapters of Romans, law (= culture) is incapable of saving anyone because it consists of works (= norms and values to be followed) which any person can only partially fulfill, hence the knowledge of standing accused (= knowing what is wrong) or having a defense (= knowing what is right) for one's actions. This is a dilemma in which any person in any culture finds himself. The only way out is not by law/culture but by faith in Jesus Christ, for by faith a person is counted righteous (i.e., having lived up to the norms and values of law/culture) by God. Law/culture is good (= functional in that society is maintained) but it also makes legal demands which no person can keep in their entirety (i.e., dysfunction occurs and the social system is not maintained). Accordingly, law/culture must make provision for punishment, a prospect which snares everyone in its net. The end result is condemnation by means of law/culture.

The Good News in the midst of this dilemma, however, is that God has intervened providing a different way by which a person can do what is right other than that according to law/culture. This very provision from God, which was forecast by prophets in Israel, is sufficient rationale for proclaiming faith in Jesus Christ among every *ethne*, cultural group, in the world. To summarize, then, God will judge each person, both Jew and Gentile, according to the law/culture available to him (+ "the light of nature", Romans 2:14, NEB), but obeying this law in its entirety is beyond what any person has done or evidently wants to do, hence salvation can be accomplished only through faith in Jesus Christ.

Now how does this understanding of cultural relativity, as illustrated in the above interpretation of Romans 1:14-16, help the missionary of today solve the problem of incorrect cultural interpretation? There are five points, which we may conclude from this discussion, that should help.

1) *God has created cultural diversity.* Just as God created diversity in physical nature, so has He created different cultures. This is the significance of the Tower of Babel in Genesis 11. Even though the immediate reason for dividing up the people building the Tower into different language groups was one of punishment, God is still the one responsible for it. In other words, God and not Satan is the source of cultural diversity. Moreover, it is God's will that cultural diversity be preserved because a) unity among men is through faith in Jesus Christ and not through any one culture (whether Jewish or otherwise), so that b) on the day of Judgment the promise of people from every cultural group standing before the throne of the Lamb (Rev. 7:9) will be fulfilled.

2) *Any individual can experience only a portion of the diversity we find in the world.* This is true both from the standpoint of all the cultures in the world and of any individual in a single culture. Of the former, for example, the vast majority of individuals in the world are monocultural, e.g., Americans are Americans, Japanese are Japanese, etc. Very few gain experience in two or more cultures. Even within a single culture an individual gets to experience only part of what is available, e.g., men cannot experience what women experience (sex changes notwithstanding, as witnessed by the fact that when men who undergo operations to become females still do not experience menstruation, pregnancy, and the pain and joy of childbirth!), and vice versa. The more complex a society, the smaller the

portion any individual can experience in terms of occupation, knowledge, lifestyle, etc.

3) *We must allow the freedom for different portions to be selected and experienced by different people and societies.* Again this is true both on the cultural and individual level. In fact, this is the significance of the running argument that Paul had with the Judaizers. The Judaizers wanted to deny the validity of any cultural experiences other than their own to Gentile believers. Paul's side of the argument, of course, was that the Gentiles were free from Jewish cultural experiences. On the individual level, this was also the significance of Paul's statement that there is no male or female in Christ. A woman, even though she may be in a culturally inferior position, need not experience the world of men to find favor before God. In short, no one society can contain all possible aspects of God's creation for its members to experience.

4) *All societies, and cultures, suffer in one way or another from the effects of sin and the Fall.* This is the significance of the coming of the Kingdom of God to earth and being established in the form of local congregations of believers. The church in the midst of society is a judgment upon the inabilities and failings of culture to make society's members truly righteous. Moreover, any one society will suffer only a portion of all possible effects of the Fall, so different societies will exhibit different shortcomings. As a result, the church in each society will have to address itself to a different set of circumstances over which the church stands in judgment, both positively and negatively, as the Kingdom of God.

5) *The nature of revelation, or the Bible, is not that of a list or text of propositions but a message to be communicated in and through social context.* The main emphasis in evangelism must be on communication and not on theologizing. The main goal of the latter is the formulation of propositions derived from revelation; their communicability in social contexts is of secondary importance. In communication, however, the emphasis is on making the content of the message relevant sociologically.

To sum up: Truth, including what the Scriptures reveal about sin, is more than what any one society or culture can contain. So to state that truth is relative to the cultural context is to claim nothing more than than that in any one context we are dealing with only a portion of what is true in this fallen world that has been graced by God's revelation of Himself. A paraphrase of Francis Schaeffer (1968) is appropriate here. Schaeffer states that God has revealed sufficient truth, but not exhaustive truth, about Himself and the world. There are truths about the world we do not know, but neither do we really need them in order to know the God who is there. In our knowledge about God we deal with only a portion of the truth on what there is to know. Similarly, when a missionary moves from his own culture to another, he should expect to be working not with exhaustive and complete truth which all cultures share but with only a portion of the human experience.

A lot of space has been taken up in discussing the issues surrounding the missionary in his role as interpreter of culture. This discussion was needed, though, because of what the missionary brings, due to prior socialization, to the task of cultural interpretation. This socialization, as we have seen, includes inputs from both the missionary's social background and his theological training. Together, they influence the missionary's cognitive processes, perhaps even laying the basis for his own cognitive style in interpreting the world. Unfortunately, they may also establish for the missionary his own paradigm for communicating the Gospel in another culture. Nevertheless, in covering this large amount of territory (and all too briefly), we have, I believe, extracted two benefits. First, such a discussion helps the missionary to *know* what he brings, both culturally and theologically, to the task of cultural interpretation and, because of this better knowledge about himself, can be in a better position to interpret cultures other than his own. Second, which is of more immediate and practical value, this excursion into cultural relativity, truth and epistemology helps define the interpretive skills needed in cultural interpretation. In this respect the missionary must be able to *relate* structure/form with its actual function(s) in society. With skills of this type at his disposal the missionary can at last engage in *correct* cultural interpretation and accurate communication of the Gospel in other social contexts.

FROM INTERPRETATION TO COMMUNICATION

Social matrices are devices from which a missionary may meaning for the purpose of understanding the culture of a society. While this is an essential preliminary step in communication, it must not be confused with the actual task of communication itself. Communication, especially cross-cultural communication, is a much more comprehensive task involving, first of all, several dimensions which, because of their very nature, cannot be included in matrices. One such dimension, as we just saw, is the role of the missionary as interpreter in cross-cultural communication. Still earlier, in Chapter III, we saw where the role of the hearer, as interpreter of the missionary's communication, is another important dimension. In brief, if a missionary is to become a cross-cultural communicator of the Gospel, he will need to do more than compile social matrices for understanding culture!

Eugene Nida's (1960) model of cross-cultural communication is well-known. The essential components of his model are 1) source, 2) message, and 3) receptor plus an arrow leading from source to receptor (e.g., S— M— R) to indicate the process of communication. Figure 4 diagrams how these components come together in a model to characterize what takes place in cross-cultural communication of the Gospel. The triangles represent the source, in this case the Bible. The Biblical message was communicated in a particular context, a fact symbolized by enclosing S— M— R, respectively, in triangles. The square represents the missionary as messenger and that he himself has received the Biblical message first of all in his own social and cultural context, a situation symbolized by enclosing S— M— R respectively in squares. The circles represent the mission or receptor culture and the fact that the Gospel as transmitted by the missionary is received in still a third context, a fact symbolized by enclosing S—M— R respectively in circles.

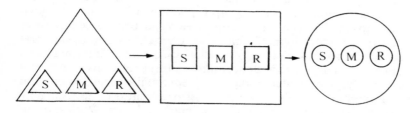

Figure 4

As diagrammed, Nida's model highlights certain features which are important in communicating the gospel cross-culturally, viz., what is being communicated by a missionary in another culture comes from a still different culture and time. As such, Nida's model emphasizes the *differences* (the triangle, square, and circle) among the three contexts in which the missionary's communication of the Gospel takes place. While such differences surely need emphasizing, they are not the whole story; other factors must likewise be highlighted before we can gain an adequate understanding of cross-cultural communication.

At this point we ourselves must admit that any model created to include these other factors will itself be inadequate; no matter how comprehensive a model might become, there will still be factors, some perhaps quite important, not included. Consequently, a model must be selective, emphasizing those factors which appear most crucial to the process the model intends to characterize. With this caveat firmly in mind, let us specify those factors needed in a model of communicating the Gospel cross-culturally.,

What are the crucial factors in cross-cultural communication which in turn must be characterized in a model? Up to this point we have been dealing with the following factors:

1) The *message,* more precisely the content that along with details of social organization becomes encoded into a message;
2) The *communicator*, especially in his role as encoder of content and interpreter of culture;
3) *Social organization*, including social institutions, functions, and social change, and how such form the basis for encoding and interpreting messages;
4) The *receptor*, or interpreter, of the message.

Also, implicit in the discussion up to now has been a fifth factor:

5) *Feedback* from the receptor to the communicator in the process of communication.

Feedback is an essential component in missionary communication in that it is an extremely crucial dimension in the correct interpretation of culture. Since cultural interpretation, as we have noted, is essentially a computational process (computing how type of society, social institution and function interact to establish the culture of a society), what the missionary is actually doing in this case is making a hypothesis of how these various factors do indeed interact and what effect such an interaction produces in a society. On making such a hypothesis the missionary tests it by encoding a message on such a basis as though it were true, communicating the message in society, and then evaluating the results. If such a communication produces, for example, adequate understanding of the message, then one's computation or hypothesis can be assumed correct. But before a missionary can come to this assessment, there must be feedback from the person or persons who receive his message. What form feedback takes place at this point (a nod of the head, eyes light up, inattention, etc.) is immaterial; the important thing is for feedback to occur.

These five factors, then, must be included and characterized in a model of cross-cultural communication. Figure 5 is an extended version of Nida's model modified to include these factors. As in Nida's model the triangle, square, arrows, etc. display the various dimensions involved in cross-cultural communication. Starting with the triangle on the left, and reading to the right, communication begins with a source, in this case the Gospel, which is to be communicated. Since the Gospel was first communicated nearly 2000 years ago, the missionary must rely on a one-way interpretation of the Gospel for the purpose of communica-

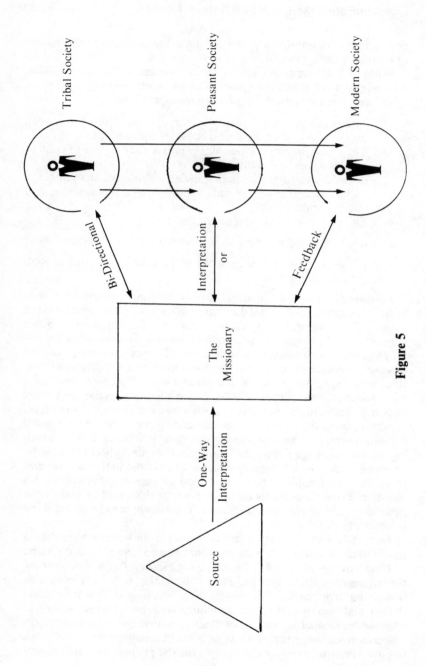

Figure 5

tion; the missionary cannot rely on feedback (i.e., *personal* interaction with the social context of Jesus' time to arrive at a understanding of the content of the Gospel) as he can when interacting and communicating with people in a contemporary society.

This one-way interpretation from the biblical source results in the missionary *selecting* (depending on his theological training, personal belief, etc.) from the source what is content and what is not content, the former constituting the essentials of the Gospel that must be communicated and the latter those details of social and cultural packaging necessary for the original communication of the Gospel in its Jewish context. This interpretive or selection process results in something different (although not necessarily unscriptural) as it becomes formulated in the person of the missionary. This difference is represented by the rectangle in the model. The rectangle also symbolizes the communication of the Gospel in and for the missionary's own sociocultural context. The choice of a rectangle to symbolize this "contextualization" is not without significance. On the one hand, the missionary's own society and culture are different than what are found in biblical times; consequently, the biblical message must be communicated in a way that will truly communicate God's will in and for the society of which the missionary is a member.

On the other hand, the missionary has the task of communicating the Gospel in other societies. In the model above these societies are represented by circles (here broken to signify that the Gospel is addressed first to the individual in society and only secondarily to the society). As the missionary has learned to communicate the Gospel in his own social context, so now he is faced with communicating the Gospel in social contexts other than his own (a situation not unlike the proverbial square in a round hole!). These circles also symbolize the differences, not only from the missionary's own social context, but also the differences from the biblical social context (represented by a triangle) in which the Gospel was first communicated. Placing the missionary (symbolized by a rectangle) in between the biblical source and the receptor societies is significant in still another way. In a real sense the missionary must *mediate* the biblical source so that the Gospel can be understood by people in the respective receptor societies. The missionary stands as God's *hermeneutes*, or interpreter, in society.

The bi-directional arrows in the model, between the missionary and the receptor societies, represent three important aspects of communication: cultural interpretation, encoding a message, and feedback. As the missionary mediates the Gospel for communication, he first makes an interpretation of the culture in which the Gospel is to be received so the Gospel can more readily be understood by people of that society. Next, the missionary encodes the Gospel in a medium (usually language) for communication. Lastly, the missionary evaluates his cultural interpretation and strategy of encoding the Gospel message by means of feedback from those who receive his communication. Adjustments may then be made at this point if any of these three aspects prove unproductive, or even counterproductive, and the Gospel is communicated once more. In this respect the bi-directional arrows also represent an important process in the task of communication, viz., a (continuous) cycling of cultural interpretation, encoding and feedback in communication. If the missionary is to ultimately make the Gospel "clear as [he] ought to speak" (Col. 4:4) in another social context, these three aspects must be "recyclable." Only by recycling can new strategies for communicating the Gospel more clearly be formulated and implemented.

To the right of the bi-directional arrows are lined drawings of individuals each of whom is enclosed in a circle. Each circle represents a type of society (tribal, peasant and modern) and the individual represents a person of that society. The arrows leading from one circle to another represent social change: for example, the arrow leading from the topmost circle to the middle circle represents a tribal society undergoing social change becoming in the end a peasant society dependent upon an elite society. Other types of social change represented in the model involves both tribal and peasant societies becoming modern. Actually, to be more precise, we should speak of individuals in tribal and peasant societies making the transition to peasant society and/or to modern society. In developing countries, which these arrow in reality signify, a missionary will more likely find individuals and not whole societies who are making the transition into the modern world. The ramifications of this observation for communicating the Gospel in today's world will be discussed in Part II.

TYING IT ALL TOGETHER

To sum up: The whole array as found in Figure 5 symbolizes the world which the missionary faces in his role as communicator of the Gospel. He is an interpreter of both the Word of God and the world in which the Gospel must be communicated. The world, however, is more complex than what is often realized. There are different types of societies each of which make different demands on individual members in terms of how the world should be organized. In addition to sociological demands imposed on individual members of society, individuals are also interacting with these demands. Some individuals, of course, conform to a high degree with these demands while others conform to a lesser degree. But regardless of the degree of conformity it is to these individuals that the Gospel is addressed. Accordingly, the missionary must formulate his communicative strategy to take into account how individuals may respond, as based on their individual interactions with their own social contexts, to his message.

The objective of such a communicative strategy is to encode the content of the Gospel in a form or message that will enable a person of another society to understand the Gospel and thereby be able to make a decision for (or against) Jesus Christ. Such an encoding, of course, must draw attention to the content of the Gospel—

> Now I would remind you, brethren, in what terms I preached to you the Gospel . . . For I delivered to you as of first importance what I also received, that Christ died for our sins in accordance with the scriptures, that he was buried, that he was raised on the third day in accordance with the scriptures (1 Cor. 15:1-4)

and not to its sociological packaging. Encoding the Gospel sociologically is necessary, just as it was necessary originally for the Jewish social context and for every other social context since. But it is the Gospel, and not its sociological packaging, that has power to save. It is on this basis that individuals of other social contexts must be able to decide for Jesus Christ.

How we may achieve this objective in today's world will be the topic of Part II.

Part II

The Missionary Faces New Religions
(What Good Is Religion, Anyway?)

Chapter 5
Religion In Society

The high value placed on individualism in western society has in similar fashion fostered an individualism in the practice of western Christianity. This individualism is found even in the mass evangelistic techniques currently popular in western Christianity, because in mass evangelism the call for conversion to Jesus Christ is made on the basis of individual or personal decisions for Christ and only after a personal experience of conversion is the person urged to join a congregation. When such an individual decision is made it is often viewed as a more "spiritual" decision than one made on the basis of family or group influence.

In many respects we must realize that this emphasis on individualism in Christian conversion is a necessary response to the more general emphasis on individualism in western society. As the functional load of maintaining society has (historically) shifted from the social institution of religion to other social institutions in western society, religion has become more personal than societal in nature. This shifting has resulted in the secularization of western society. If the Gospel is to gain any hearing in western secular society, it must be via individualism.

While individualism is a valid strategy for communicating the Gospel in western society, the same strategy can produce some unexpected side-effects if used in communicating the Gospel in other social contexts by western missonaries. The first effect is that individualism (both as a cultural value and evangelistic strategy) may establish the hermeneutic by which the western missionary interprets other cultures: as religion is unimportant societally in the missionary's own context, so is it judged unimportant societally in the new culture. Now this may indeed be true for the new cultural context, but then again it may not be. In either event, the western emphasis on individualism may lead the missionary to downplay the role and benefit of religion as a social institution. A second side-effect may be the missionary calling for individual decisions for Christ without regard to how decisions (religious or otherwise) are actually made in the receptor society. There the ideal type of decision may not be individually based but a decision that takes into account what other members of the group think. Perhaps the most unexpected

side-effect is the reinforcement that individualism, as the cultural hermeneutic of the western missionary, provides in the secularization of
nonwestern societies. Secularization is spreading to other societies as
well, resulting in greater emphasis on individualism in each case. The
western missionary, with individualism already a category in his scheme
for cultural interpretation, merely speeds up the secularization process
by calling for individual conversion to Christ.

This is not to pass a judgment on the secularization consequences of
the missionary's communication of the Gospel in nonwestern societies.
Indeed, secularization is probably inevitably in today's world, even
without help from western missionaries, because of mass communication, technology, western education, Marxist ideology, etc. On the other
hand, the above may be considered a judgment on carrying individualism as a strategy of communicating the Gospel over into a social context
where individualism is not highly regarded. If individualism is carried
over into such a society, it becomes encoded (whether unconsciously or
by design) in the message of the Gospel and is thus picked up by
members of that society perhaps as an essential component to be
accepted in converting to Christianity. Again, this may be suitable for
the receptor society, but if religion in the receptor society happens to be
important *societally* and not just important individually, then members
of that society may interpret the Gospel as being irrelevant for them in
their social context. In such a case Christianity may very well be rejected
because it does not fulfill certain societal expectations deemed necessary
by society's members.

A similar interpretation of the Gospel message, when based on
individualism, is made by nonchristian people in western society, i.e.,
nonchristians also pick up the notions that the Gospel is unimportant
societally. While this may be a valid method in evangelism in western
society, it must not stop here in the total communication of the
Gospel, because even in western society there must be more to
evangelism than waiting to find a person in a vulnerable moment
psychologically at which time the Gospel is communicated as the
source of personal integration. The Gospel has ramifications for
western society as well as for the individual.

The above introductory remarks lead to the main emphasis of this
chapter, indeed the whole of Part II. That emphasis is the need, for
communicating the Gospel cross-culturally, of considering religion in its
social context and not only in terms of belief. Religion in society has
largely been a neglected dimension in missionary communication while
religion as belief has received the major emphasis. This neglect must be
corrected and a better balance between religion as a social institution,
performing societal functions, and as a system of belief must be
achieved. This chapter begins this rebalancing showing why religion in

its social environment is a necessary dimension in the task of communicating the Gospel in an understandable manner cross-culturally.

SOCIOLOGY OF RELIGION

In Part I we emphasized that religion as a social institution is primary in communicating the Gospel cross-culturally. This emphasis is to be understood in two senses. First, of all five social institutions, religion plays the greater role in cultural interpretation and planning one's strategy for communicating the content of the Gospel in a new cultural context. Second, which is equally important for our purposes, religion as a social institution takes precedence over religion as a system of belief in cultural interpretation and planning a strategy for communicating the Gospel in a new cultural context. This is a different emphasis than what has normally been the case. Normally, in religious studies for missionary communication, the focus is on belief and comparison of beliefs among religions. The reason for this emphasis appears to be this: since belief is considered the most important aspect of Christianity, it is assumed that any point of contact with people of other religions must be at this level. Implicit in this assumption is still another assumption: as belief is the most important category in (western) Christianity, so is belief equally important as a category in other religions. Because of these two assumptions, when religions are compared, the emphasis is on comparisons of belief with little thought given to comparing the sociological dynamics that religion may exhibit from one cultural context to another.

Belief, of course, does not remain equally important or constant in intensity from one religion to another, or from one society to another. Some religions, for example, are more pragmatic while others are more doctrinaire; still others are open to assimilating new rituals and beliefs while others are closed to outside influence and change. Religious belief, in other words, will vary in importance and in intensity from one society to another, a factor which ultimately makes comparison of belief systems unproductive for our purpose of cultural interpretation and planning communication strategy. Only by comparing religions sociologically can a comparison be productive for these purposes.

There are four reasons for this emphasis on the social aspects of religion in this book on cross-cultural communication.

The first reason is because religion is functional in society. Religion helps to maintain society and plays an important role in forming the cognitive map through which members of society make sense of the world, including the message of the Gospel preached by the missionary. That religion is functional in these two ways in tribal and peasant societies is apparent. For modern society, where the functional role of religion has shifted from the societal to the individual, the picture is more complicated. Nevertheless, religion in modern society still plays a crucial role in forming the cognitive map (even if it is in a negative way) for society's members (more on this below).

The second reason is that conversion to the Gospel message is as much sociological as it is theological. Donald McGavran was one of the first to emphasize the sociological aspects to conversion:

> Rational, denominational, and theological factors certainly play a large part in the conversion of men everywhere, but so do environmental factors of which an important instance is this one that Eurican Christians see with such difficulty: that men like to become Christians while remaining within their own people, without crossing social barriers. (1970:208)

People want to see how the Gospel is relevant to their social life. If the Gospel is communicated without taking into account social relevancy, the Gospel may not be accepted.

The third reason for emphasizing the sociological side to religion over religion as a system of beliefs is that belief, more often than not, is made to accommodate social reality. Religious beliefs are often modified or reinterpreted to support a change in social policy or behavior, becoming in the end rationalization for the new reality. Now this is not to advocate that such should be the case, but it is a recognition of where nonchristian man (plus many Christians!) is in regard to belief and social reality. The communicator of the Gospel must not uncritically assume that his listeners hold a similarly high view of belief, or that they are motivated to act first by religious belief and only secondarily by social behavior. But by realizing the equal, if not greater, role that society plays in shaping how people believe, the Gospel communicator can plan more effective strategies for calling men to belief in Jesus Christ.

The fourth reason for making religion in society primary in this book is that the Gospel message must affect society as well as individuals. Of course, the Gospel is addressed to individuals, but in our communication of the Gospel we must not neglect to spell out the ramifications of the Gospel for living in society. This holds true obviously for the church, because the church consists of believers living socially with others in God's kingdom.

> Therefore, putting away falsehood, let everyone speak the truth with his neighbor, for we are members one another (Eph. 4:25).

But it is also true for Christians living as members of society in general:

> Maintain good conduct among the Gentiles, so that in every case they speak against you as wrongdoers, they may see your good deeds and glorify God on the day of visitation (1 Pet. 2:12).

One's strategy for communicating the Gospel in today's world must not stop with personal salvation for the individual but must also include how the new faith is to be lived in society. Only by faith being lived in society can the Gospel have an effect in society.

RELIGION: THE PRIMARY MATRIX

Earlier we stated that social matrices are devices that a missionary may use for interpreting and understanding another culture. There are five such social matrices, one for each of the five major social institutions of society. But of the five matrices we also stated that the social matrix describing religion in society is the basic hermeneutical device for the missionary in the important task of interpreting culture. In this section we will construct a social matrix for religion which may be used in cultural interpretation.

Figure 6 is such a matrix for religion. It is constructed to take into account two important dimensions crucial for the interpretation of culture: type of society and the function of religion as a social institution in society. Three types of societies are represented in the matrix: tribal, peasant, and modern. Three ways in which religion may function to maintain society are also represented. The first way is termed *holistic*, i.e., religion as a social institution interrelates with every other social institution on a more or less equal basis for maintaining society. The second way in which religion may function in society is termed *compartmentalized*. Compartmentalization is, in effect, the opposite of holistic: religion is no longer interrelated with other social institutions contributing its fair share in maintaining society. Rather, religion is more "compartmentalized" from the other social institutions, being

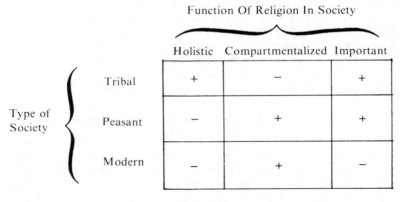

Function Of Religion In Society

Type of Society		Holistic	Compartmentalized	Important
	Tribal	+	−	+
	Peasant	−	+	+
	Modern	−	+	−

Figure 6

made in the process more highly visible as a separate institution. The third way in which religion functions in society is in *importance*, a function more fully explained below. It must be remembered at this point, however, that importance in the matrix above refers to the importance of religion societally and not individually or personally.

The two dimensions of type of society and function of religion intersect to provide us a characterization of religion in society. Figure 6 also shows the intersection in terms of plus + or minus - in each square of the matrix. The function of religion in tribal society is [+ holistic] but [-compartmentalized], i.e., religion as a social institution interrelates more or less equally with all other social institutions in maintaining tribal society. Obviously, if religion functions holistically in tribal society, then it is also [+ important]. The function of religion in peasant society, on the other hand, is [-holistic] and [+ compartmentalized]. Religion in peasant society does not function holistically with other social institutions in maintaining society but must share its functional load with the corresponding social institution of elite society. But even if religion is compartmentalized in peasant society it is nonetheless [+ important] for the maintenance of peasant society, for it is important societally in peasant culture in terms of entertainment (as in religious festivals), life crises and transitions, and also in the legitimization (hence, a comfort) of the current position that peasants must occupy in the social order vis-a-vis elite society. Finally the function of religion in modern society is [- holistic], [+ compartmentalized] and [-important]. While religion may be important individually it is not important societally. This importance in maintaining (modern) society is now carried by the social institutions of government and economics.

The pluses and minuses in Figure 6 serve in two additional ways. First, they characterize religion in each type of society, hence providing a cultural interpretation of each society in terms of the function of religion. Second, the pluses and minuses serve to differentiate one type of society from another. For example, tribal society differs from peasant society in that religion is [+ holistic] for the former but [- holistic] for the latter. Peasant society, in turn, differs from modern society in that religion is [+ important] for the former but [- important] for the latter.

VARIATION IN FUNCTION AND COMMUNICATION STRATEGY

The function of religion varies from one type of society to another. Consequently our strategy for communicating the Gospel should also change for each type of society we encounter. As the social functions of religion change from one type of society to another, so should our communication strategy. The reason for this should be obvious. If, for example, a missionary from a modern society encodes the Gospel message in terms of [- holistic + compartmentalized - important] for proclamation in a tribal society, the Gospel may be rejected because members of the society may be trying to interpret the message in terms of [+ holistic -compartmentalized + important], i.e., how the Gospel may "fit in" with and support other areas of their social life such as government, economics and education. Of course, if no "fit" is discerned, the Gospel may be considered irrelevant for their social situation. To avoid this adverse interpretation, the missionary should change his communication strategy to communicate, in addition to the content of the Gospel, how the Gospel is relevant societally for tribal people.

Communication strategy, in this sense, is very similar to what we may term evangelistic thrust. Different societies or different segments of society require different thrusts or emphases in evangelism. We would not expect, for instance, to use the same evangelistic methods in urban New England as we do in rural Texas (although some evangelists do!). Rather, we would ask such questions as: what aspect of the Gospel do we emphasize for each type of society? or, what portion of the Gospel will "strike home" first in each type of society? Different emphases, in other words, must be made for different types of society. Now this may seem contrary to the universality of the Gospel, but we must remember that we are not referring to the content of the Gospel when discussing these concepts. We are referring to changes of thrust and strategy in communicating the content of the Gospel.

The Bible, more precisely the □iblical message, is capable of such changes in thrust and emphases. The Apostle Paul realized the Gospel's flexibility in this regard during his missionary journeys. On his second journey, as a case in point, he circumcised Timothy because his mother was a Jew (Acts 16:3), but during the same period of time Paul refused to have Titus circumcised because Titus was a Greek (Gal. 2:3). The church in Jerusalem was also concerned with the need for flexibility in evangelistic thrust among the Gentiles (Acts 15). Such flexibility, of course, became the hallmark feature of Paul's preaching, of becoming all things to all men so that he might win some (1 Cor. 9:19-23). The modern missionary must in the same manner be capable of changing emphases and thrusts in proclaiming the Gospel in other societies.

At this point an assumption underlying our discussion should be made explicit, viz., how we "structure" our evangelistic thrust carries *information* in addition to the content we proclaim. The very emphasis we build into the thrust communicates additional information to listeners. Just as the type of package containing a gift communicates information (e.g., about the value or importance of the gift), so does the "package" in which the content of the Gospel is wrapped communicates information about the Gospel. As result, then, if a missionary has the wrong emphasis or "packaging" for the Gospel, for the type of society he is in, problems in misunderstanding the appropriateness of the Gospel may arise.

This principle is also seen in the way society is structured in terms of social institutions and their functions. Tribal and peasant societies are [+ important] with respect to the function of religion in society. This amounts to an emphasis, or thrust, in each society that communicates information about religion in addition to its teachings, myths and rituals. Even the [- important] for religion in modern society communicates information, because the fact that religion is not important societally is just as pervasive in modern society as [+ important] is for religion in tribal and peasant societies. If the Gospel is to gain a hearing in society, in other words, it must speak to the emphasis or thrust that religion has in that society. This, of course, requires flexibility on the part of the communicator and evangelist to plan different strategies to meet different social emphases.

Communication strategy or evangelistic thrust is not only concerned with "fitting in" with the particular emphasis of each society. As was implied in the introduction to this chapter, communication strategy is also concerned with the *goal* of communicating the Gospel in other social contexts. This is because God has something to say to each type of society. This statement may be a judgment upon the emphasis of the society, or it may be a reinforcement of an emphasis. For example, if at all possible we would not want our preaching in tribal and peasant societies to weaken the importance religion has societally for these societies and thus promote an individualism that may be contrary to the emphasis found in these societies. Likewise, we should not want to be found guilty of perpetuating and reinforcing individualism (e.g., "solo" Christianity) in modern society. Our goal in proclaiming the Gospel, then, should be maintaining the importance of Jesus Christ for tribal and peasant societies and pointing out how Jesus Christ must affect life holistically in modern society.

LOOKING AHEAD

We are now ready to get into what I consider the heart of this book, preaching the Gospel in different types of societies. Specifically, over the next four chapters, we will investigate the various strategies and emphases a missionary may take in communicating the Gospel in a tribal society, a peasant society, a modern society, and in a developing nation where elements of these main societal types come together to form a continuum of change from the tribal to the modern. We will investigate in more detail the various societal types involved and explore the types of emphases and thrusts that may be taken by a missionary in preaching the Gospel.

In a real sense we will be investigating the *potential* contained in the Scriptures for communicating the Biblical message in today's world of different types of societies. The potential of the Scriptures is so much greater than what any one type of society can explore and assimilate. This, I believe, is what the Apostle Paul meant when he referred to the grace that was given him "to preach to the Gentiles the unsearchable riches of Christ" (Eph. 3:8). We who are westerners have assimilated only part of what is available in Christ, but if we desire to preach the Gospel to other nations, we must, along with Paul, have the

> power to comprehend with all the saints what is the breadth and length and height and depth, and to know the love of Christ which surpasses knowledge, that we may be filled with all the fullness of God.
>
> Now to him who by the power at work within us is able to do far more abundantly than all that we ask or think, to him be glory in the Church and in Christ Jesus to all generations, for ever and ever. Amen. (Eph. 3:18-21)

Today's world is complex, but within the pages of the Bible there is still the "breadth and length and height and depth"—in short, the potential—for every person of any type of society to know the love of Christ. We must comprehend this potential, or "fullness", and be capable of communicating it fully in today's world. The following five chapters are dedicated to that end.

Chapter 6
Communicating The Gospel In Tribal Society

Phat had a request to make. It was the cool season (December) in the mountains of northern Thailand and time to cut the trees and brush on a mountain side in preparation for planting the next year's rice crop. But before he could begin cutting, he had to perform a ceremony to inform the *sooy*, spirit, that inhabited the mountain side that he had chosen the site for his rice field. He would have to build a small dwelling place (the size of a bird house) at the edge of the site and ask the *sooy* to live there until the rice was harvested and transported back to his home in the village. Then the spirit would be invited to reinhabit the site.

As a member of Mal tribal society, Phat had grown up to perform this ceremony every year. Otherwise, he believed, the *sooy* of a site would be disturbed and angered by the cutting, burning and planting, and in retaliation would destroy the rice crop. Without informing the *sooy* first of one's activity, according to the knowledge of the Mal, rice would wither and die in the field. It was impossible to dispense with such a crucial ceremony—unless, of course, some other ceremony or power could accomplish the same purpose of causing a *sooy* to move from a site.

Phat had been listening to my discussions on God's power over the *sooy* or spirits. Consequently, he called me aside one day to make his request. "Teacher, can you go and pray in my rice field in order to expel the *sooy*? I don't want to perform the usual ceremony for this again this year."

I assured Phat I would be happy to pray in his rice field, asking God to expel the *sooy*. I also assured him that God would answer this prayer but I also had a warning. Unless Phat himself would become a Christian, praying to God continually to keep the *sooy* away from his rice field, the *sooy* would return after I had left and the results could be worse than before (cf. Mt. 12:43-45). Phat thought a moment on this and decided the cost was too high. There were too many social and family pressures against him becoming a Christian. Under these circumstances it was better to continue performing the traditional ceremony.

This chapter explores the ramifications of communicating the Gospel in tribal society. In more precise terms we will examine those details of tribal social organization that should be encoded along with the content of the Gospel so individuals in tribal society can understand the message of the Gospel and make decisions based on the relevancy of the Gospel's content to their own social context. The above brief interchange, from my experience among the Mal tribe, illustrates some of these details of tribal social organization. As can be seen, communicating the Gospel in tribal society touches on areas of social life other than just religion.

RELIGION IN TRIBAL SOCIETY

Religion in tribal society is usually characterized as animism. The term animism was introduced by Edward B. Tylor in his book *Primitive Cultures* first published in 1871. Tylor's purpose in coining the term was to provide the beginning point in his theory describing the evolutionary development of religion. The great religions of the contemporary world, Tylor contended, evolved from the time when man first perceived nature to be "animated." From this beginning man next conceived the separation of the "animated" part from nature itself thus resulting into the existence of separate spiritual beings. It was from this belief in spiritual beings that marked the real beginning of religion. Tylor's evolutionary theory, however, did not survive the coming of the 20th Century (E. E. Evans-Pritchard 1965). On the other hand, his term animism survived as a description of the particular type of religious belief found in tribal societies.

Animism is more than a belief in spiritual beings. There is one other essential component to animism, viz., along with the belief in the existence of spiritual beings there is also the belief that these spiritual beings are in control of the operations of the phenomenal world, at least in control of that part of the world considered important for human existence and survival.

Of the two components essential to animism, the second is probably the more important in understanding animism. For example, the number of spiritual beings, or how complex their relation to each other, appear immaterial in characterizing animism. The Mal believe in the existence of numerous spirits, but they fall in only two categories, the spirits of dead parents and all other spirits. Even the spirits of dead parents, once the children have also died, get reclassified into the second category by grandchildren whose major concern now are the spirits of their parents. Other tribal societies, of course, have extensive belief systems consisting of ghosts, demons, spirits, gods, mythical creatures arranged in complex hierarchies of power and authority. But what really distinguishes animism from other types of belief systems, even those that believe in the existence of spirits, is the doctrine that nature is under the control of spiritual beings. Plants grow or die and humans live or become sick because of spirits. For man to have food and remain healthy he must live in harmony with these controlling forces. When the food supply fails or he gets sick it is evidence that he has angered the spirits that are in control. To make things right during such times, man must perform ceremonies and bloody sacrifices. These will appease the offended spirits and restore nature back to its normal operation (cf. David Filbeck 1964).

The belief that spiritual beings are in control of the physical world is equally important for understanding the function of animism in tribal society. Following the matrix of Chapter 5, we see that animism functions holistically, i.e., animism as the social institution of religion interrelates with every other social institution in forming and maintaining tribal society. Indeed, animism is such a pervasive belief that it does more than just interrelate with other social institutions: animism is the source of integration and cohesion in tribal society, the "linkage" that links one social institution with another. All other institutions, in other words, function in society on the basis of animism. If animism fails to do its part in maintaining society, it is perceived that all other institutions must likewise fail resulting in the disintegration of society.

Let's examine more closely some of the major ways animism is the integrating force for tribal society. Keep in mind that in animism spirits are in control of the operations of nature. Since each social institution deals with at least some aspect of the normal operations of nature, we can see animism providing the explanation why such operations, regardless of the social institution involved, sometimes go awry.

Animism and Economics. Economically tribal societies are directly dependent on the earth producing an adequate amount of food. Food may be obtained from the earth by means of hunting, foraging, fishing, agriculture and raising domesticated animals. Many tribal societies employ all five methods to gain enough food for survival. Under such circumstances there is rarely a surplus of food stuff, a condition needed for the development of a more complex economic system in society. On the other hand, trade and barter of perishable food stuff do occur in tribal society thus creating more to economics than simple exploitation of the earth's resources. Other aspects of life—clothing, tools, housing materials etc.—also enter the economic stream of life. Nevertheless, it is food that remains of utmost concern. Accordingly, it is food and its production that is the focal point in the relationship between animism and economics in maintaining tribal society.

Not every type of food becomes the concern of animism in tribal society, however. For the most part only the main staple of the tribe becomes the focal point of animism. For example, in a society that depends on hunting wild game for its staple food, animism will focus on assuring a good supply of game and success in killing. For the Mal and other tribal societies of Southeast Asia, rice is the staple, and consequently assuring an adequate harvest is the main concern of animism. Whatever type(s) of food is the staple in a tribal society, animism functions to assure normal operations in nature so there will be an adequate supply for survival. "Normal" in this case means that it is the natural function of the earth to produce food. As long as food is being produced, animism has little function to perform. But nature does not always operate normally; animals disappear, hunting is unsuccessful, rice dies in the field, etc. It is at this point, when such disruptions occur, that animism functions in tribal society. First, animism provides the explanation for the disruption and, second, it specifies what needs to be done religiously to restore nature back to normal operations so food will again be produced in adequate supply. In animism spirits cause such disruptions. They have been angered, often because a member of society has broken a taboo and they are now disrupting nature to punish the member. Certain ceremonies and sacrifices are in order to appease the spirits, thus allowing nature to return to its normal operations.

In a number of tribal societies there are also other aspects in the relationship between animism and food production. *Magic* and *mana* are two such items and are similarly important in understanding animism. Magic, for instance, is often used in a manipulative manner to assure that nature does indeed operate normally in her task of producing food. Mana, on the other hand, or more properly viewed as "power" (sometimes personal, at other times impersonal) inherent in the operational process of nature to produce food. When the food supply fails to meet an adequate level of production, the cause for such failure is then traced back to the wrong type magic performed, or to a lessening in the amount of mana nature. If the former is the case, then the right magic must be performed properly, and if the cause is the latter, then ceremonies or sacrifices must be performed to increase the level of mana in nature. Both serve the purpose of restoring nature back to her normal production of food.

Animism and the Family. The relationship of animism with family, in the maintenance of tribal society, occurs at the point of tension between personal health and illness. This is not difficult to understand when this aspect of life is related to the economics of food production. A person must be well and healthy to hunt, fish, plant and harvest a crop, etc.; otherwise, it is impossible to obtain the food needed for survival. Moreover, if the person is a spouse or parent responsible for obtaining and preparing food for a family, the relationship, more precisely the interdependency, among the three looms all the more crucial in the task of maintaining society. In the case of animism and the family, therefore, the normal operations of nature consist of each individual being healthy and free of illness. When a person is ill, which occurs all too often in tribal society, nature is not operating normally. Animism functions at this point in providing the explanation for the abnormal operations. A spirit has been angered, perhaps by the sick person having broken a taboo, and the spirit is now punishing the person by making him sick. Animism also functions by outlining the ceremonies and sacrifices needed to appease the spirit in order to restore nature back to normal operations, i.e., to regain one's health.

There are other points of contact between animism and the family in tribal society. Some of these include building a new house, birth, adolescence, marriage, and death. Ultimately, however, every area of family life becomes linked to food production at the point of tension between health and illness. The ceremonies, feasts and sacrifices that occur when a new house is built, a birth, a marriage, etc., are performed to assure one of two results: a healthy life free of illness or to prevent beforehand the spirits from becoming angry and visiting the people involved with illness. When life is lived free of illness, obtaining an adequate amount of food is assured.

At this point it is also not difficult to understand why a family's ancestral spirits are important spirits in animism. At death, in animism, a person becomes a spirit (ultimately, it appears, all spirits in animism were formerly humans; but this is an ontological, perhaps theological, questions that need not concern us). Moreover, in animism, kinship ties and obligations are not dissolved when death in a family occurs. A kin, upon dying, stays a member of the family, and the family is expected to take care of the deceased kin, providing a place in the house for the kin to dwell and placing food on a regular basis at this place for the kin, who is now a spirit, to eat. In return the deceased kin is to do his part by assuring that life for the living proceeds normally. Consequently, if a living member of the family becomes ill, one of the first places to look for the cause of the illness is one's own ancestral spirits. If an ancestral spirits proves to be the cause of the illness, the afflicted member must perform certain ceremonies to appease the ancestral spirit to regain his health.

Animism and Government. In tribal society animism and government become related in the area of social control. This relationship also ties in with food production and the tension between health and illness. In animism it is perceived that just as there are (ancestral) spirits that belong to the individual and his kinship group, so are there spirits that belong to the society. And just as one's ancestral spirits affect food production and health for the kinship group, so do the spirits of the society affect the general level of food production and health of all of society. Accordingly, there are rules and regulations (taboos) that all members of a tribal society must follow. If a taboo is broken, then all of society, and not just an individual or kinship unit, suffers: a blight, for example, may spread throughout the main food crop of the society, or an epidemic may strike down and incapacitate a large section of society's members. When such social calamities occur, the cause is traced to the spirits of society being angered and punishing all of society.

To avoid such social misfortunes from occurring (they occur all too often in tribal society), and to assure that life proceeds normally, members of society must be kept in line. At this point, religious leaders in animism (shamans, priests) come to exercise a great deal of power and political control over society, because they are the ones who know the taboos and the effects upon society if they are broken. Accordingly, religious leaders often have great authority in enforcing strict adherence to the taboos by all members of society. Among the Mal, as a case in point, publicly coming to blows in a fight between two or more members of society is a village taboo. When such occurs, the spirit over the village is angered and will punish the village by sending an epidemic of fever to run its course through the village population. To avoid this calamity from occurring, the village shaman fines the combatants and requires all villagers to participate in a sacrifice to appease the spirit.

It is in the area of government that some tribal societies make a distinction between demons and spirits, or spirits and gods, or minor spirits and major spirits, etc. Lesser spirits tend to be an individual's or family's ancestral spirits controlling only the fortunes of the kinship group. Major spirits or gods tend to belong to the social group controlling in turn the fortunes of the group. On the other hand, tribal spirits or gods are not normally perceived as being universal in power and scope, i.e., as being gods over other tribes as well; other tribes have their own spirits and gods, and the spiritual beings of the various tribes do not traffic with each other except perhaps in time of war. In tribal warfare the tribe that wins may be considered as having the more powerful deities, and the tribe that loses may have to submit to the control and taboos of the deities of the victorious tribe.

Many tribal societies have concepts of a supreme deity who is universal in some sense, e.g., as creator of the earth. However, this supreme deity is normally not associated with having control over food production and health; hence, there is no necessary reason to include the supreme deity in the governmental task of social control. As a result, few if any taboos are associated with the supreme deity and he goes largely forgotten as people cope with staying healthy in order to obtain an adequate amount of food for survival.

Animism and Education The point of relationship between animism and education lies in the rich variety of rituals, ceremonies, and festivals found in animism. These are public occasions and have been appropriately termed drama in anthropology. As implied earlier in this section, the major function of these rites is to assure that nature for the maintenance of society is the socialization of the oncoming generation so it, too, will know the forces that control so much of people's lives and what must be done to keep nature operating normally. In short, education, through the visual aid of drama, functions to socialize children in the animistic culture of society. As rituals and ceremonies are performed, children watch; when festivals are staged, children are incorporated and soon learn their role. By these means the next generation of adult members assimilate what is needed to assure an adequate of food and health.

To sum up this section: Animism, as a social institution, forms the basis of interdependence among the social institutions, in tribal society. It is this basis that gives tribal society its holistic character. More importantly for our purposes, though, is that animism, as the ground of social integration and cohesion, establishes the context for communicating the Gospel in tribal societies.

HOLISM AND POWER ENCOUNTER IN TRIBAL SOCIETY

Duang announced one evening that he was leaving Christianity and reverting back to his animistic beliefs and customs. I had met Duang on my first visit to his tribal village. He was nearly blind from a severe eye infection when I first saw him, so I invited him to return home with me for a couple of weeks in order to treat his eyes with antibiotics. His wife led him to the Thai market town where I lived at the time, and after two weeks of daily treatment, the infection in his eyes cleared up and he regained a measure of sight. While they were around the house, we talked about Jesus Christ and what faith in Him meant. It wasn't long after returning to his village that Duang and his wife were baptized.

The reason for returning to animism, Duang explained, was pressure from his parents. A few days earlier a cow belonging to his parents wandered off in the forest and could not be found. The parents concluded that the reason the cow had not been found or had not returned on its own was because Duang had become a Christian. On becoming a Christian Duang had ceased to perform any of the ceremonies and sacrifices necessary in animism. This particularly angered the ancestral spirits of the family, his parents said, because it means that Duang was not fulfilling his kinship obligations to take care of deceased kin. In punishment, therefore, the family's ancestral spirits caused the cow to wander away. Furthermore, the parents argued, the cow would not return unless Duang recant his new faith and return to fulfill his obligations toward his ancestral spirits.

Under intense pressure from his parents Duang agreed to recant; no amount of counter argument on my part was persuasive enough to prevent him from leaving Christianity. He and his wife immediately announced they no longer were Christians, and soon afterwards the cow that belonged to his parents returned to the village.

The preceding illustrates what Alan Tippett (1973) has termed the *power encounter* in communicating the gospel in other cultures. To Tippett the concept of a power encounter is an encounter between the Christian and the kingdom of Satan. Since Satan has power, he exercises authority over men who in turn become enslaved to Satan's power. The Christian's encounter with nonchristians, therefore, must also be with power and authority, viz., the power of Christ because all authority has been given to Him. Mere presence or a silent witness through good works is insufficient power to break Satan's power over men. Only by taking the offensive against Satan's kingdom will the Christian break Satan's hold over men.

In tribal society the power encounter that Tippett describes takes place on two levels. First, there is the encounter between different belief systems regarding the ultimate power lying behind the operations of nature. But more importantly is the power encounter that takes place on the social level; indeed, it is in the social arena that the power encounter in tribal society is played out in its most intense form. It is one thing to decide on the merits of different beliefs, but it is quite another matter to implement a belief in life. What happens in life tests one's faith in extreme ways. This, of course, was the arena where Duang encountered the demands of the Gospel. The animism of Duang's society functioned holistically, even to the extent of explaining why a family cow would disappear in the forest. Because of the holistic nature of animism, it was also perceived in this society that Christianity similarly extended to all areas of life and is not confined to some autonomous region of social life called religion. For Duang and his parents, then, the issue was simple: which contained the power to return the cow? To Duang's parents there was only one such power, viz., their ancestral spirits.

There is another dimension to the power encounter in communicating the Gospel in tribal societies. Not only is there a power encounter between the Gospel and society, there is often a power encounter between the missionary's conception of power in today's world and the concept of power in animism. We must remember that there may be a difference between what the Scriptures say about power and what a (western) missionary, in his role of interpreter, conceives that power to be or what it might and might not cover in today's world. As has been emphasized many times in this book, a message is encoded on the basis of how society is organized. In the case of the western missionary, then, unless he is otherwise sensitive to the different way tribal society is organized, he will encode the Gospel message with respect to power in terms that reflect the mechanistic view of nature that western society has come to adopt. That is, God has "wound up" the cosmos which is now operating on its own with little interference from God. Occurrences, such as illnesses, bad crops, or missing cows, are explained in naturalistic terms. Because of a mechanistic view of nature, God's power is divided by westerners into two types: His power as manifested through the (mechanistic) workings of the universe and His power to save and "keep to the uttermost" those who trust Him.

This concept of power, and its subsequent encoding for communication by the western missionary, is due to the social changes that have occurred in western society, viz., the shifting of functions for maintaining society that religion at one time performed to other social institutions. This change has resulted in a secularization of western society and in turn has established the cognitive map for understanding power. So in encoding and communicating the Gospel on the basis of a secularized cognitive map, the Gospel in effect does not cover all that it should—indeed, all that it must!—in order to be effective in tribal society. In fact, the power encounter, which Tippett claims to be essential in conversion, does not take place in tribal society under such circumstances.

To effectively communicate the Gospel in tribal society, a missionary must encode the Gospel message on the basis of the way tribal society is organized with respect to power, i.e., on the basis that the operations of nature are under the control of spirits. Now encoding the Gospel on such a basis is not foreign or contrary to the Scriptures. For example, the *Logos* of John 1:1 was no doubt understood by many in New Testament times as referring to that power that sustains the cosmos. While many probably considered the *Logos* as an impersonal, hence unspiritual, power, there is no doubt that the New Testament writers regarded the *Logos* as personal and spiritual, existing in the person of Jesus Christ.

> In many and various ways God spoke of old to our fathers by the prophets; but in these last days he has spoken to us by a Son whom he has appointed the heir of all things, through whom also he created the world. He reflects the glory of God and bears the very stamp of his nature, *upholding the universe by his word of power* (Heb. 1:1-3 RSV).

The Apostle Paul also accents this theme in his Epistle to the Colossians, an epistle, incidentally, that is excellent for understanding the true nature of the power encounter between the Gospel and animism. Regarding the nature of the power that sustains the created world, Paul wrote

> He [Jesus Christ] is before all things and in him all things hold together (Col. 1:17).

As in animism, the Scriptures assert that the natural world is under the control of spirit.

71989

Therefore, the power encounter that must take place as the Gospel is communicated in a tribal society is not one of an encounter between the western mechanistic view of nature versus animism; rather, the encounter is over *who* is in control of the operations of nature, Jesus Christ or one's ancestral/tribal spirits? From this perspective, the main issue in the power encounter between the Gospel and animism is over the question of allegiance: Shall one's allegiance be to Jesus Christ or to one's ancestral/tribal spirits as the controlling power over the operations of nature? Paul realized that this was the real issue in the church's encounter with "the powers":

> For we are not contending against flesh and blood, but against the powers, against the world rulers of this present darkness, against spiritual hosts of wickedness in the heavenly places (Eph. 6:12 RSV).

All the above suggests the goals the missionary should have in communicating the Gospel in tribal society. There are two such goals. First, in terms of understanding, individuals in tribal society must understand that the "bottom line" to the operations of nature is still spirit but that spiritual being is Jesus Christ. Second, in terms of persuasion (2 Cor. 5:11), the Gospel is communicated with a view of persuading individuals to *change allegiance* from their ancestral/tribal spirits to Jesus Christ as the one who is in control of nature.

> For he has made known to us in all wisdom and insight the mystery of his will, according to his purpose which he set forth in Christ as a plan for the fullness of time, to unite all things in him, things in heaven and things on earth (Eph. 1:9-10 RSV).

"ALL THINGS SHALL BE YOURS AS WELL"

How shall the preceding two goals be achieved? What communicative strategy shall we use to achieve the type of understanding and change of allegiance among individuals of tribal society as outlined above? Another way of asking the same question is this: What is the potential of the Scriptures in communicating the Gospel in tribal society?

Obviously, the Bible has within it the potential for achieving the above two goals of communication in tribal society. The problem, when there is one, of not seeing that potential lies more with the western missionary who does not come from a tribal society and thereby interprets God's communication (the Bible) to us on the basis of another social context. Because of the way western secular society establishes the cognitive map for interpreting the supernatural side of the Bible, the western Christian has a marked tendency to overlook the potential of the Scriptures for proclamation in any type of society other than his own.

We have space for examining only a couple of examples of the Bible's potential for tribal society. We shall investigate them from the standpoint of their strategic importance in producing in tribal society the type of understanding and changes in allegiance necessary for conversion to Jesus Christ.

The first example is taken from Matthew 6:25-33.

> Therefore I tell you, do not be anxious about your life, what you shall eat or what you shall drink, nor about your body, what you shall put on. Is not life more than food and the body more than clothing? Look at the birds of the air: they neither sow nor reap nor gather into barns, and yet your heavenly Father feeds them. Are you not of more value than they? And which of you by being anxious can add one cubit to his span of life? And why are you anxious about clothing? Consider the lilies of the field, how they grow; they neither toil nor spin; yet I tell you, even Solomon in all his glory was not arrayed like one of these. But if God so clothes the grass of the field, which today is alive and tomorrow is thrown into the oven, will he not much more clothe you, O men of little faith? Therefore do not be anxious, saying "What shall we eat?" or "What shall we drink?" or "What shall we wear?" For the Gentiles seek all these things; and your heavenly Father knows that you need them all. But seek first his Kingdom and his righteousness, and all these things shall be yours as well. (RSV).

The significance of this text for communicating the Gospel in tribal society is three-fold.

First, this text addresses the basic concerns of animists in conversion, viz., if they believe in Jesus Christ they will be forsaking the spiritual powers that keep nature producing food, or they will anger the spirits who in turn will cause nature not to produce food. By becoming Christians, animists often fear, they will face starvation. However, this text can alleviate that concern because it shows that God provides food for us.

Second, this text shows that God is the *active agent* in the operational processes of nature. For example, God is actively engaged in feeding the birds and in causing flowers to grow (as "clothing" for the grass of the field). This is an important point to establish in an animistic society. God is not far removed from us but is the source of what nature produces. It is not the ancestral/tribal spirits who are the source of food. Not only is God the source for nature producing food, but he also knows beforehand that we need food. God is actively engaged in causing nature to produce, even before we need it, the food we need.

The third significance of Mt. 6:25-33 for communicating the Gospel in tribal society is the judgment that these verses pronounce upon tribal society. The priority in tribal society is the production of an adequate supply of food for survival. This priority, however, leads to forgetting God and looking to ancestral and tribal spirits for assurances in obtaining food from the earth. But priority in life must not be food as in animism but upon God's kingdom and His righteousness. It is not enough, in other words, to accept God as Spirit and in control of nature. Tribal society must also place His kingdom first. Only then will "All these things . . . be theirs as well."

The second example of the Bible's potential for tribal society is taken from James 5:13-18.

> Is any one among you suffering? Let him pray. Is any cheerful? Let him sing praises. Is any among you sick? Let him call for the elders of the church, and let them pray over him, anointing him with oil in the name of the Lord; and the prayer of faith will save the sick man, and the Lord will raise him up; and if he has committed sins, he will be forgiven. Therefore confess your sins to one another, and pray for one another, that you may be healed. The prayer of a righteous man has great power in its effects. (RSV)

This text addresses the second basic concern of animists, illness. God, who is in control of the operations of nature, also heals. But in addition to this point the text also points out two dimensions of healing significant for communicating the Gospel among animists.

The first dimension is the context of healing, i.e., calling for the elders of the church to pray and anointing the sick person with oil. Illness in a tribal society is not an individual matter; it is a community affair, the community being the family, tribe or both. Illness is a community matter because sickness in animism is traced back to the ancestral or tribal spirits of the sick person. Through the ancestral/tribal spirits the illness of the individual becomes related to every other member of the community. But more than this, in a subsistence economy where every person's labor is necessary for food production, to have one person sick affects everyone else because it means that the same amount of food must still be produced but with fewer workers. And as illness affects the whole community in various ways, so does the healing process. Elders and older members of the family and tribe, who know the ceremonies, sacrifices and incantations, are called upon to divine the ancestral/tribal spirits and perform the rituals that restore health to the sick person.

Communicating, along with the content of the Gospel that illness and healing are similarly community affairs in Christianity, "speaks" to the tribal context. The church is the community of God in tribal society. Those in the church who are elders and know how to pray to God are to be called in to pray and anoint with oil. The use of oil in healing in New Testament times deserves special comment here. Traditionally, the church has considered oil in James 5 as belonging to the way society of New Testament times was organized for healing; it did not belong to the content of the Gospel. As a detail of New Testament social organization used in healing, oil may be compared (in the communication process) with what is used today in healing.

The second dimension to healing contained in James 5:13-16, significant for animists, is the connexion made between sin and sickness on the one hand and between forgiveness and health on the other hand. In tribal society the same connexions are also made. When a person becomes ill, for instance, the illness may be traced back to the person having offended an ancestral or tribal spirit, a concept of sin not dissimilar to the biblical term transgression. For healing, then, the offended spirit "forgives" the offense and the healing process can begin.

A word of (exegetical) caution is needed here, however. While sin and sickness, and forgiveness and health, are related in James 5, and such relationships certainly "speak" to animists in tribal society, there are significant differences between the Scriptures and animism at these points of similarity. Sin in the Bible is not merely "offending" God, nor is illness the automatic response from an offended god. Sin and disease have deeper roots than what animism can reveal. But while this is true, it must not be forgotten that the two are ultimately related in the Scriptures. And if the missionary is to communicate the Gospel in tribal society sin and disease, as well as forgiveness and health, must be kept related, not only because this is the nature of tribal society and animism, but also because the same relationship is made in the Bible.

THE GOSPEL AND SOCIAL CHANGE IN TRIBAL SOCIETY

Of all societies a tribal society is perhaps the most vulnerable to social change as a result of the Gospel. This is due in large measure to its holistic nature, i.e., how animism and all other social institutions are tightly interdependent in forming and maintaining tribal society. Any intrusion from the outside into a tribal society will often produce change not only at the point of intrusion but through other parts of the society as well.

The first type of social change that occurs in tribal society is the "institutionalization" of social institutions. Institutionalization may be understood as the highlighting of a social institution by means of emphasis and the presence of specialists, to where it becomes isolated from other institutions. In the contact between the Gospel and tribal society, religion is usually the first to undergo this highlighting effect. This is unavoidable because of the character and emphasis of missions. How much institutionalization of religion (i.e., isolating religion from the rest of society and creating a corps of specialists) actually takes place in tribal society depends on the communication strategy used in addressing the two main concerns of animists, an adequate food supply and health.

There are two alternatives in addressing these concerns of tribal society. One is addressing them institutionally, and the other is addressing them holistically.

In the short history of modern missions, the two concerns of food supply and health in tribal society have traditionally been addressed institutionally. For example, concerning the problem of assuring an adequate food supply agricultural specialists and techniques have often been introduced. With fertilizer, hybrid seeds, and improved breeds of livestock, all under the control and guidance of Christian specialists, food production has been increased, sometimes dramatically so. To assure continued good health of people in tribal societies, modern medical personnel and techniques have similarly been introduced. With the building of hospitals and outpatient clinics, along with introducing vaccines, antibiotics and vitamins, again under the control of Christian specialists, the general health of the tribal population improves. Furthermore, to assure continued improvement in these areas for the next generation, schools were established to use these new techniques in agriculture and health. And as the students grew up to become adult members of society, they were able to assume many of the specializations (educator, agriculturalist, nurse, etc.) held by missionaries.

Unfortunately, this institutionalization, where it has occurred in a tribal society, while addressing the twin concerns of food and health, often has had an indirect but profound effect on the communication of the Gospel to nonchristian animist members of society, an effect, moreover, that extends to neighboring nonchristian tribal societies as well. As health, agriculture and education are receiving special emphases, for example, there occurs a corresponding separation of these areas of life from religion. This development means that the training of future church leaders (who are also being trained along with teachers, agriculturists, nurses, etc.) in the schools is now restricted to certain religious things more western than tribal in orientation. Consequently, once trained, the new generation of church leaders, who should be prepared to communicate the Gospel to nonchristian animists of their own society and even beyond to neighboring tribal societies, actually have nothing to say. Their strategy of addressing the main concerns of animists is too institutionally bound to be relevant for anyone except the Christian of their own society. The net result in communication under such circumstances, then, is a turning inward to build up the church spiritually. Evangelism among animists largely ceases and the church stops growing except for the addition of children born to Christian parents.

The second alternative in addressing the major concerns of tribal society is to address them holistically, i.e., to show how Christ affects all of life and every social institution, and beyond that to show that all things are summed up in Christ (Col. 1:17). The Scripture texts of the previous section addressed the concerns of food and health in a holistic manner. The discussion revolving around these texts was designed to show their potential in achieving two important goals in communicating the Gospel: understanding the relevancy of the Gospel for the tribal social context and persuasion in terms of this relevancy. As animism relates to every area of life, so should Jesus Christ. As people in tribal society are able to relate to each other by means of social institutions based on animism, so should they be able to do the same by means of Jesus Christ through the church.

Obviously, by addressing the concerns of tribal people holistically, institutionalization in tribal society can be kept at a minimum. This does not mean that no change takes place, however, because even by virtue of the contact with Christianity, things are never the same for people in tribal society. If nothing else, at least their life experiences and language have expanded to take into account the contact. The fact that social change occurs because of contact with Christian missions should not cause concern. In this age contact with the outside world is unavoidable for any tribal society located anyplace on the earth's surface. If missionaries have not entered a tribal society yet, anthropologists and government officials most certainly have.

The main question, therefore, facing Christian missions in communicating the Gospel in tribal society is this: How much social change should the communication of the Gospel produce in tribal society? or, What direction should social change take in tribal society? Should our strategy for communicating the Gospel lead a tribal society to where social institutions become highlighted and eventually separate from each other in the daily life of tribal people? Or should our communication strategy strive to integrate Jesus Christ into every area of life thus showing His relevancy for all social institutions of society? Given the holistic nature of tribal society, plus the relevancy of Jesus Christ for every area of life, the Gospel message must similarly be organized and structured for communication in and for tribal society.

Chapter 7
Communicating The Gospel In Peasant Society

There are more than two billion peasants in the world (Oriol Pi-Sunyar and Zdenek Salzmann 1978)—fully one-half of the world's population! The size of this population alone commands that we give serious attention to the task of communicating the Gospel to peasants.

Who are the peasants of this world? Traditionally, scholars have termed them rural cultivators, but as George M. Foster (1967:6) states, this is too restrictive.

> Like most anthropologists, we agree that peasants are primarily agriculturists, but we also believe that the criteria of definition must be structural and relational rather than occupational. For in most peasant societies, significant numbers of people earn their living from nonagricultural occupations. It is not *what* peasants produce that is significant; it is how and to whom they dispose of what the produce that counts.

There is another, more contemporary reason for broadening the definition of *peasant*, a reason moreover that equally demands our attention in communicating the Gospel in today's world. In recent years large numbers of rural peasants have fled to the urban centers of the world. A few peasants who migrate to the city do manage to find adequate employment, but the vast majority end up living in slums, shanty towns or ghettos subsisting on the meager wages gained from manual labor. In reality their status in society at large has not changed from their former rural peasant background. They can rightly be called "urban peasants", because in a real sense they form a part-society subordinate to a more powerful urban elite.

Both rural peasants and their urban kin will be the focus on this chapter. Sociologically, both share many features in common. Of course, the urban environment creates a number of different conditions not present in a rural environment. These differences, however, as they relate to communicating the Gospel cross-culturally, will be discussed later in Chapter 9. Here we focus on those common features involved in communicating the Gospel to people, whether in a rural or urban setting, who must live in a dependent and surbordinate relationship with an elite and powerful segment of society.

There are two more factors, outside of population and setting, why we should pay special attention to peasants as a social type. The first is the fact that many tribal groups, formally autonomous and self-sufficient, have been brought into a dependent and subordinate relationship to more powerful central governments. That is, these groups have been made into peasants; their social institutions no longer function holistically but must function under the oversight of more powerful institutions of the dominant society. Short of government collapse, this dependency will not be reversed; rather, we can expect in the future more tribal groups to be made dependent to central governments thus increasing the peasant population of the world even more.

The other factor for paying special attention to peasants as a social type is the similarity between peasant society and biblical society. If there is any one social type that more closely resembles biblical times, especially the social context of the first century Palestine, it is peasant society. Realizing this similarity can help the missionary in two ways in the task of communicating the Gospel in peasant society. First, it can help the missionary relate more directly the biblical message to peasant society of today. As the mediator between the Gospel and the social context wherein the Gospel must be communicated, a missionary in a peasant society is able to encode the content the Gospel on a sociological foundation that contains several more points of similarity to the biblical context than either tribal or modern society. Correspondingly, if properly done, the resulting message will be interpreted by members of peasant society in terms greatly similar to New Testament times.

Second, realizing the sociological similarities between peasant societies of today and New Testament times can help the missionary define the Gospel message for a large section of the world's population. As we shall see later on in this chapter, there is alot of controversy over what should be the message of the Gospel for that half of the world who are peasants. But, if the social context wherein Jesus of Nazareth preached was peasant in character, then how He encoded the Good News of the Kingdom for first century Palestine should serve as the model for communicating the Gospel cross-culturally in peasant society today.

PEASANT SOCIETY: A CHARACTERIZATION

In Chapter II we first introduced peasant society as a part-society dependent upon and subordinate to an elite segment that stands in control of all society. This initial description, however, was only a beginning point in characterizing peasant society. Peasant society, even as a part-society, is much more complex. In this section we will present a more detailed picture of what peasant society is like.

At the outset it should be realized that peasant society is not comparable to rural society in America. There are a number of important differences between the traditional peasant and the American farmer. For one thing, all the trappings of modern society are available to the latter. As a result, farming in America has become more economically oriented. Farming is no longer just agriculture, it is now agribusiness. Land is considered in terms of yield-per-acre, or in grazing capacity of n-number of cattle. A farmer may rent ground, even living as a tenant on the rented ground, but his tenancy is calculated in terms of turning a profit. It is farming, moreover, as distinguished from peasant agriculture, that is assuming a greater role in maintaining society in today's world. With the world population increasing each year, the food produced by the agribusiness of modern society is increasingly needed to feed the world. Peasant agriculture, because of its lack of mechanization, fertilizers, etc., is not able to produce enough to feed a growing world population.

We initially characterized peasant society as part-society. But what does this mean? It was an anthropologist, A.L. Kroeber (1948:284), who first observed: "Peasants are definitely rural—yet live in relation to market towns; they form a class segment of a larger population which usually contains urban centers, sometimes metropolitan capitals. They constitute part-societies with part-cultures." Robert Redfield (1956), while following Kroeber in this definition, also characterized peasant society as "intermediate between the tribe and the modern city", as having an "up-and-down relation to more primitive tribal peoples, on the one hand, and to towns and cities, on the other."

It was Eric Wolfe (1966), however, who described in detail what part-society means in relation to peasants. His description is based on the economics of the peasant situation and involves the dimensions of surpluses, power in distributing surpluses, and the peasant adaptation to the use of that power. Wolfe states that the peasant, as all cultivators, is concerned with producing enough food to feed his family plus a surplus which may be sold or traded for other necessities of life. The peasant, though, must also contend with a dominant elite who hold the power to demand a part, if not all, of the peasant's surplus for redistribution to nonfood producers. The peasant, in his position as a member of a part-society is therefore subject to an asymmetrical power arrangement which extracts payment. The return for this payment, in the form of government services (police, bureaucrats, etc.), is often considered on the part of the peasant greatly inferior to the value of the surplus taken. Yet, there is little the peasant can do in the face of such power and exploitation except to adapt and survive. One way in which peasants may adapt, Wolfe states, is to consume surpluses in performing ceremonies, by staging religious festivals, etc. Since such surpluses will be taken away in any event, peasants figure they and not government officials should consume the surplus food. Consequently, festivals and other events are frequently staged. A second way to adapt to the asymmetrical power arrangement is to curtail both production and consumption. This way there will simply be no surplus to take!

One point should be reemphasized here. While most peasants are rural cultivators, peasant society as a social type should not be restricted to a rural population. Other types of population may also be included in the social type. The basis of inclusion is the dependency of the population on a more powerful elite. Where such dependency exists, whether it is rural-urban or slum-city hall, a common set of characteristics (attitudes, behavior, etc.) is also found. Even though examples of the peasant situation in this chapter are for the most part taken from rural settings, it should be remembered that they exemplify a *subordinate relationship* and not necessarily a rural-urban relationship. The peasant condition is found in environments other than rural.

The asymmetrical power relation between peasant population (whether rural or urban) and an elite population produces a type of culture that is distinct from the cultures that emerge either in tribal or modern society. This distinctiveness, in the words of Oriol Pi-Sunyar and Zdenek Salzmann (1978) forms a way of life for members of peasant society, a way of life that results into a personality type that is distinctively peasant. Pi-Sunyar and Salzmann describe twelve cultural features that are characteristic of peasant society and which in turn form the outlook on life that peasants have. Because these characteristics are basic to understanding peasant society let us briefly summarize each one.

Agriculture is a means of livelihood, and not a business for profit. Robert Redfield (1956) stresses this feature even more. He states that the peasant has an intimate and reverent attitude toward the land and that agricultural work is good while commerce is not. This is true even for nonagricultural peasants, e.g., fishermen and herders. The means of subsistence often becomes a livelihood, a (family) tradition, that oncoming generations are expected to follow. To break with this means of livelihood is to break away from a sacred tradition.

Peasants experience many insecurities in life. The source of such insecurities is not a fear of producing an insufficient amount of food from the land. This is real enough. However, the main source of insecurity in peasant life is the subordinate position peasants must occupy in society. Even if food production is adequate there is the real threat that a large share will be taken away by the more powerful of society. And even when food production is not adequate, because of drought, insects, etc., there is still the chance that a larger portion will be expropriated thus creating real deprivation. As a consequence, peasants often fear and distrust outsiders (e.g., agricultural specialists, medical specialists, religious teachers) who have a genuine desire to help. It is, after all, other outsiders, in the form of tax collectors, land owners, etc., who come to extract their share of the peasant's labor and wealth.

Ceremonialism creates heavy financial demands. Earlier we noted that ceremonies and festivals are adaptive mechanisms in the peasant's power struggle with the elite of society. By consuming surpluses in religious activity, peasants may prevent the tax collector and landowner from collecting a greater share than usual. But there is more to ceremonialism than this. Since religion in peasant society, as described in chapter V, is [+ important], great effort is directed at meeting the material demands of religious observances. For such observances new clothes are often purchased, additional food is bought, large amounts of alcoholic beverages are made or bought, all of which require great outlays of money that may place additional financial strains on individuals and families. Nevertheless, since such expenditures are deemed necessary, peasants will sacrifice and endure deprivation to meet the demands of ceremonialism.

Peasants often exhibit in their lifestyle a lack of deferred gratification. There is a marked tendency among peasants to spend money as they get it instead of saving in order to enjoy the buying power that a large sum of money brings. This "lack of deferred gratification", as economists term it, stems from the insecurities that peasants undergo because of their subordinate position in society. If their money is to be taken away through taxation, rent owed to the landlord, and the demands of ceremonialism, there is little incentive to save. It is better to spend it now; at least one may enjoy the fruits of his labor even though it is a small amount.

Peasants emphasize personal relationship over impersonal, contractual relationships. In any type of society both personal and contractual relationships occur. But since the relationship between peasants and the elite of society is mainly contractual, peasants grow to distrust such relationships. It is the elite, in the perception of peasants, who are the more powerful and who are all too prone to use that power to exploit the relationship to their benefit. By preferring personal relationships, on the other hand, peasants feel they can control the outcome more to their benefit. In personal relationships mutual obligations between the participants are established. These obligations function much like a bank account: whenever help or aid is needed, a peasant may "draw" upon the account by requesting assistance from those who are obligated to him. In a contractual relationship all such obligations are discharged immediately at the time of transaction; no more assistance can be expected.

Peasants tend to be distrustful. This feature of peasant culture has already been mentioned above. Yet, distrust appears to be such a pervasive feature of peasant personality that it is singled out here for special emphasis. Peasants enter each relationship with the suspicion that the other party will exploit the situation to his advantage. Only as a relationship grows into a personal one, where mutual obligations become firmly established, will suspicions cease. But outsiders and the elite of society do not normally enter into personal relationships with peasants. In this case suspicion quickly turns into distrust, a trait that a peasant may carry with him in all his dealings with outsiders.

Peasants tend to believe that there is only a limited amount of good to go around. The earth can produce only so much of the good things of life. The good, therefore, must be fairly and justly distributed among all members of society. If a person appears to be getting wealthy, then it is perceived that he is receiving more than his fair share of the good thus depriving other members of society from receiving what rightly belongs to them. Moreover, it is often believed that wealth (i.e., one's more than fair share of the earth's good) is obtained by deceit and manipulation. Consequently, peasants often consider the rich deceitful, unjust and immoral. Such a view of the rich feeds and reinforces the distrust that is characteristic of peasants. The concept of limited good also breeds jealousy and envy among peasants themselves, because whenever fellow peasants harvest a higher yield of grain or have more pigs to survive an epidemic, others perceive his good fortune as receiving more than his fair share of good. To bring him back into line, part of this grain may be destroyed or some of his pigs poisoned.

Peasants give greater importance to family ties than to any other type of relationship. Obviously, when a peasant feels insecure, distrustful and envious, there is only one place to turn: his family. At least there, because of the mutual obligations among members that a family creates, one can find security, trust and understanding.

Special obligations are placed upon the peasants who are more wealthy. Despite the concept of the limited good and the leveling effect this has on the accumulation of wealth, there will still be some peasants who will have more than others. Consequently, if those who have more do not wish to earn the distrust and approbation of their less fortunate neighbors, they must be willing to share in times of need, to make loans at the beginning of the planting season, to hire at harvest time, and to be patient in collecting debts. Otherwise, those who are more wealthy may suffer vandalism and destruction of property, perhaps ending up with having lost more than if they had fulfilled their special obligations. In a real way these obligations upon the wealthy serve the function of redistributing wealth in society and thus keep feelings of suspicion and envy in check.

Peasants feel they are essentially powerless in society. The elite and rich of society, by obtaining more than their fair share of the earth's goods, have also captured more than their fair share of power. In a real sense this is true, because wealth is power; it demands respect for those who have it. The opposite is just as painfully true: poverty is powerlessness and invites only disdain from the wealthy. This sense of powerlessness often creates an attitude of resignation on the part of peasants. There is only one thing, it seems a peasant can do: make the best of a bad situation. And if worse comes to worse . . . well, it is God's will being carried out.

Peasants are noted for their religious fervor. This stems directly from their sense of powerlessness. Without power in this world there is only one place to turn: religion. Faith that heaven is ultimately on their side sustains through poverty. Hope that something better lies beyond this life propels peasants to endure hardships. But while religious fervor may be commendable, it also has its negative side. While faith and hope may promise a better afterlife, they may also produce a fatalism toward the conditions of life in this world, i.e., a feeling that nothing can be done to change and improve life now. For this reason peasants may turn very conservative, even working against those who seek to improve their lot on earth.

Peasants are also noted for perpetrating the bandit mystique as another way of coping with their powerlessness. Robin Hood, of course, is the most famous example of this trait. The function of the bandit mystique, however, appears to be more communicative than real. Its message is directed toward the elite of society: if a minimum of justice is not forthcoming, then the elite will have more than just bandits on their hands. They will face a peasant revolt, perhaps even a revolution, that will overthrow the elite and transfer their power to the peasants.

Even though the bandit mystique serves as warning to the rich and powerful of worse things to come, there have been few peasant revolts and even fewer peasant revolutions down through history. There have been peasant protests and insurrections over the centuries, but for the most part they have been leaderless and directionless. Their aim was usually to redress immediate grievances and not to effect any long range change in the social system. After grievances were aired and solutions agreed upon, conditions returned to normal, the peasants continuing with their lifestyle and the elite continuing with their power. Because of this underlying conservatism even in times of protest, revolutionary leaders have often bypassed peasants in favor of the proletariat (the urban working class) in the task of redistributing power in society. Karl Marx, for this reason, held few sympathies for peasants. As a result, it became a point of orthodoxy in Marxism that the revolution which would usher in the communist state would be the work of the urban working class. Mao Tse-tung, however, because China was not industrialized and therefore had no proletariat, mobilized peasants to carry out the communist revolution in China. This was considered heresy by Marxist purists and finally was an important aspect in the division between the communist parties of Russia and China.

While the preceding is a characterization of peasant society, thus allowing us to more adequately understand peasant culture and personality, a word of caution is needed. The characterizations should not be viewed as cultural absolutes, or that every peasant must personally exhibit the traits and attributes described in the characterizations. Rather, they must be viewed as cultural parameters that define the limits of the peasant situation. For example, within the peasant situation there will be individuals who are more distrustful than others while some will be less distrustful. Yet both degrees of distrustfulness will be in reaction to the powerlessness of the peasant's subordinate position in society. In similar fashion some peasants will exhibit more religious fervor than others, or perhaps be more skeptical of the bandit mystique. In short, it must be remembered that the personalities of peasants will vary within the cultural parameters established by the characteristics described above. To sum up: individual peasants should not be *stereotyped* according to these characteristics but be viewed as more-or-less typical within the range they define.

RELIGION IN PEASANT SOCIETY

Some Thai peasants living in the northern part of Thailand were once asked how, as Buddhists, they saw no contradiction in also worshiping a local but powerful deity that inhabited the surrounding forest. Doctrinally there was a contradiction because Theravada Buddhism, as taught in Thailand, denies the existence of otherworldly beings as spirits (ancestors and demons), gods, devils, etc. To be an orthodox Buddhist, therefore, one should not also be an animist.

When we inquired about the Forest-Spirit we also asked questions on the relations of the villagers of Ban Pa Hung to Buddhism. In the village there is one temple built on wooden poles and covered with thatch. This temple is not much larger than the joss-house of the spirit in the forest. One priest is living there . . . We asked the villagers whether the priest does not forbid them to worship the spirit. They answered that the Buddhist religion helps a man to get merits. It teaches us to behave well and to hold the five commandments: do not kill, drink whiskey, lie, steal, and commit adultery. Hearing the teaching of the Buddha and giving food to the teacher brings personal merit. So we might pass away to a better life.

But in this life there is only the spirit who can help the poor man. How could Buddhism help to fight rats eating the rice on the stem? How can Buddhism drive wild pigs away when they come to devastate the fields? The matter of the Spirit are the business of the spirit and the matters of the temple are the business of the temple. One does not contradict nor oppose the other. (Christian Velder 1963).

This incident illustrates two sociological aspects of religion commonly found in peasant society: compartmentalization and what Robert Redfield (1965) called the Great Tradition versus the Little Tradition in peasant society.

Compartmentalization, as already implied several times in the course of this book, means that religion as a social institution is a separate and more highly visible "compartment" in society functioning in a less holistic way with respect to other social institutions for the maintenance of peasant society. In other words, the compartmentalization of religion in society is the same as institutionalization, a process briefly described in Chapter 5. Religion in peasant society becomes compartmentalized or separated from other areas of life under the impact of religion in elite society. Religion in elite society, with its highly trained specialists and doctrines expertly formulated, is already highly institutionalized. This institutionalization in turn has an effect on the practice of peasant religion, creating in its wake a more highly visible social institution than what otherwise might be the case.

But there is another dimension to the compartmentalization of religion in peasant society. That dimension is the co-existence in peasant society of two religions (or two varieties of the same religion), each one fulfilling different purposes and meeting different needs. These different purposes and needs are mutually exclusive, i.e., certain needs can be fulfilled or met by one religion but not by the other. In the example above from Thailand, Buddhism served the purpose of allowing a person to accumulate a sufficient amount of merits so that in reincarnation after death he may be born into a better and more wealthy position in life. Moreover, Buddhism permits merit to be accumulated over countless cycles of birth, death and reincarnation so one may ultimately attain Nirvana where one is absorbed into the final essence of the universe. Accordingly, it was evident that the Forest-Spirit had no such purpose to fulfill. The Spirit's purpose, on the other hand, was to meet the felt need of protecting one's rice crop growing in the field. Furthermore, it was equally evident that Buddhism had no part to play in meeting this human need. Consequently, both Buddhism and the Forest-Spirit were deemed necessary in the religious life of the Thai villagers.

This compartmentalization of two religions into fulfilling sharply different purposes leads to the second dimension of religion in peasant society, viz., the presence of a Little Tradition in opposition to a Great Tradition. The Great Tradition represents the orthodox version of a major religion (e.g., orthodox Christianity, Islam or Buddhism) while the Little Tradition represents either a folk (some would say corrupted) version of the same religion or some other religion altogether (as in the case of the Forest-Spirit in the above example from Thailand). An interesting example of the two traditions in a single society is to be found in Judaism of Palestine during the time of Jesus Christ. In John 9 Jesus healed a man blind from birth who then was brought before the Jews. The Jews, consisting of the Pharisees, the chief priests (Jn. 7:32) and the authorities (Jn. 7:48, probably the Sadducees who were in political power at the time), formed the Great Tradition in Judaism. The uneducated and common people (e.g., the Apostles, Acts 4:13), especially those from Galilee (e.g., Jesus of Nazareth, Jn. 7:41, 52), formed the Little Tradition. Because of this social difference the Jews haughtily dismissed the (former) blind man's account of how he had been healed ("would you teach us?"), accusing him of having been born in sin (a status often attributed to the unorthodox practioners of the Little Tradition). Having made this "elitist" conclusion they cast him out of the synagogue (Jn. 9:34).

Above, we mentioned that the Little Tradition may be a folk, or even corrupted, version of the Great Tradition, or orthodox version, of religion in elite society. No major world religion, it seems, is without its folk version. Alan R. Tippett (1975), for example, describes a type of folk Christianity commonly found in Meso-America. Among peasants in Meso-America elements of animistic beliefs and practices have become mixed with Christian and Roman Catholic elements into a single religion. This (new) religion has aptly been termed Christopaganism: it is neither Christian or pagan but a combination. Islam also has its folk variation in peasant areas. John G. Kennedy writes about popular and orthodox Islam among the Nubians in southern Egypt. Popular Islam centers on worshipping at the shrines of saints and on placating or avoiding evil spirits. It is in a syncretism that existed even before the Nubians were pressured to convert from Christianity to Islam in 1317 A.D. "That Nubian Christianity had been only a thin veneer over indigenous folk beliefs and practices would help to explain the equally superficial substitution of Islam as an official religion" (John G. Kennedy 1977:17).

The existence of a Little Tradition among peasants and a Great Tradition among the elite of society poses a special problem in cultural hermeneutics on the part of the American missionary serving in a peasant society. In American society orthodox or conservative Christianity is more often associated with rural and small community populations than with urban populations. The urban setting, with its more highly educated and heterogeneous population, is associated with liberal, perhaps unorthodox, Christianity. Consequently, in serving in a peasant society an American missionary may, on the basis of how his own society is organized with respect to social setting and orthodoxy, may make two interpretations. One, the peasant religious situation corresponds to the conservative Christianity practiced in American rural areas, and, two, elite society is the repository of liberal and unorthodox religious beliefs and practices.

The true situation in peasant society, however, is just the opposite. The reason for this is that orthodoxy requires a high level of education and clerical specialization to maintain. These conditions, of course, are unavailable in peasant society, thus making religion in peasant society more susceptible to folk or even syncretistic innovations. But if this situation is recognized, then a missionary can adjust his strategy of communicating the Gospel in peasant society to assure that the Gospel does not become just a Little Tradition perhaps mixed with other, nonchristian elements.

"THE COMMON PEOPLE HEARD HIM GLADLY"

The King James Version virtually stands alone in its interpretation of *ochlos* in Mark 12:37: "And the *common people* heard [Jesus] gladly". Other versions of the New Testament translates *ochlos* in this verse as "great throng" (RSV), "large crowd" (TEV, NIV), "great crowd" (NEB), etc. On the other hand, William F. Arndt and F. Wilbur Gingrich (1957), in their Greek-English lexicon, state that *ochlos* in Mark 12 means "the common people (as) contrast to the rulers, the lower class". In this context, therefore, the King James translators appeared to have had a clearer understanding of the actual social situation in first century Palestine than what many modern day translators have.

As noted in the beginning of this chapter, there are several similarities between peasant society (and peasant personality characteristics) and Palestine of New Testament times. Mark 12 is an excellent example of several of these similarities. The context for Mark 12 begins at Mark 11:27 at the time when Jesus returned to Jerusalem and was walking in the temple. The chief priests, scribes and elders (the religious elite) confronted Jesus with a question: On what authority was he carrying out His mission? Jesus countered this by asking them on what authority did John the Baptist preach, man's or God's? The religious leaders were afraid to answer because if they said God's authority, then they stood self-condemned, but if they said man's authority, they would make the people (*ochlos*) angry. Next, Jesus told the parable of the vineyard (Mk. 12:1-12), a parable directed against the religious leaders but about which they could do nothing because they feared the multitude (*ochlos*). Immediately after this, the Pharisees, Sadducees, and a scribe, in succession, tried to best Jesus in various arguments. Jesus won each argument after which "no one dared to ask him any question" (Mk. 12:34).

Jesus then "turned the tables" on His adversaries by referring to a well-known assertion about the Christ made by the scribes. The scribes asserted that the Christ was David's Son. But if this were true, Jesus went on to ask, why did David call him Lord (Ps. 110:1)? How could the Christ be both inferior (son) and superior (Lord) of David at the same time? It was a paradox that the scribes, despite their vast knowledge of the Scriptures, could not explain. The resulting discomfort suffered by the scribes (who were members of elite society in Palestine) in being bested in an argument by a Galilean, of course, was not lost upon the *ochlos*, the people who were members of the common class. In fact, the *ochlos* enjoyed the exchange, listening to Jesus gladly.

Mark 12 continues on this same vein. Jesus next condemns the scribes "who like to go about in long robes, and to have salutations in the market places and the best seats in the synagogues and the places of honor at feasts", etc. The chapter closes with Jesus looking on as the rich and poor (a characteristic difference between the elite and peasants of society) make their donations to the temple. Jesus, in His final summation of His stay in the temple, condemns the scribes for their ostentatious behavior while praising the poor who give all they have to the temple, because in the end it amounts to much more than the rich who give out of their abundance.

We are fortunate that Palestine society of New Testament times resembles peasant society of today, because by investigating how

Jesus encoded the Good News of God's Kingdom for the first century peasants of Palestine (as we briefly did in Mk. 12 above), we should be able to formulate a similar strategy for communicating the same Good news for peasant society today. Jesus faced most, if not all, of the cultural characteristics described for peasant society in the previous section. In addition, Jesus faced another characteristic that was not discussed but which is very much a part of today's peasant situation. Not only was Jewish society divided into elite and common populations, but Jewish society as a whole was also under the domination of a world power, the Roman Empire, a social situation that affected, although in different ways, both elite and common Jews in Palestine. The same conditions exist for many peasants today: not only are they subordinate to an elite segment of society, but they are also affected by world powers. How Jesus proclaimed the Kingdom to "common people" who had to live under the domination of a world power should in the same way serve as our model for communicating the Gospel under similar circumstances today.

Jesus, for example, faced in the peasants of first century Palestine a strong attachment to the land. Of course, there were from the Jewish context even stronger theological reasons for this attachment (cf. Gen. 17:8), but the outcome in society was nevertheless much the same as any other peasant society. Jesus also faced excessive ceremonialism (cf. the tradition of the elders) and distrust on the part of the common people. Because of the power of the Romans, plus the ubiquitous power of the Jewish religious leaders in first century Palestine, Jesus recognized the powerlessness of the common people. Jesus even faced the bandit mystique both among His own band of disciples (Acts 1:6) and the people in general (Jn. 6:15).

How did Jesus approach the Jewish peasant context of first century Palestine? What strategy did he use to communicate the true nature of God's Kingdom to them? Let's investigate the Gospel to discover how Jesus communicated the Good News to a peasant society of his day.

On attachment to the land. There was a special theological significance to Palestine; it was the Promised Land. Because of this there was a special sanctity to the land that all Jews recognized. Yet, the outcome of this significance was an attachment to the area that exceeded the intent of the original Covenant given to Abraham. The geographical area of Palestine and the coming Messianic Kingdom were, in the opinion of many, to be one and the same. This produced a conservatism that in turn led to a distrust of outsiders, the Gentiles, unless they would first become Jews. Jesus countered this by citing examples in Israel's history of nonjews being blessed (e.g., the widow of Zarephath and Naaman of Syria, Lk. 4:26-27), demonstrating that

God's mercy was not nearly as dependent on the Promised Land as many Jews believed. Jesus also constantly dissociated God's Kingdom from the actual land area of Palestine (cf. "My Kingdom is not of this world," Jn. 18:36), placing its location instead "among" people (Lk. 17:21).

On ceremonialism. The Jews of the first century were known for their "tradition" handed down from respected teachers of the past. These traditions were not the Law; they were interpretations or rulings designed to safeguard both the Law and the people from breaking the Law. The rationale behind these interpretations was this: if a person broke a ruling on a point of the Law, he would be transgressing the interpretation and not the Law itself. Unfortunately over time such interpretations grew to have as much authority as the Law, becoming, as a result, additional ceremonies that the Jewish people had to observe. This arrangmement caught the common people in a dilemma. On the one hand they could ill afford the burdens of excessive ceremonialism (for the most part promoted by the Pharisees), but, on the other hand, they were also afraid not to observe the extra ceremonies lest in their ignorance they might break the Law and become an outcaste. Jesus condemned this ceremonialism (Mk. 7:1-13), stating that the intent of the Law was not to create more ceremonies for observances (Mt. 23:1-4) but to assure that each person would love God and his neighbor as himself: "On these two commandments depend all the law and the prophets" (Mt. 22:34-40).

On distrust. Of all the different ethnic groups that inhabited first century Palestine, the Jews disliked the Samaritans and the Romans the most. For these two groups the Jewish dislike had also grown into distrust. The reason for distrusting the Samaritans was theological and historical (2 Kings 17:24-41), while the reason for distrusting the Romans was political. Both the dislike and the distrust displayed toward these two groups had become so intense over the years that together they formed a cultural trait in Jewish life. Jesus confronted this trait, however. On distrusting the Samaritans, Jesus told the parable of the Good Samaritan (Lk. 10:29-37), a parable whose meaning was not lost on the Jews because it showed that the Samaritans were as trustworthy in time of real human need as another cultural group. Regarding the Romans, the scribes and chief priests tried one time to exploit the distrust that the Jews had for the Roman government in order to embarrass Jesus before the common people. They asked Jesus if taxes should be paid to Caesar (Lk. 20:19-26), to which Jesus replied: "Render to Caesar the things that are Caesar's and to God the things that are God's." No distrust, in short, even though motivated by theological, historical or political reasons, was to be a part of God's Kingdom.

On powerlessness. Proclaiming the Kingdom of God in an atmosphere of powerlessness was perhaps the most difficult task Jesus faced in first century Palestine. For one thing, Jesus had to proclaim that God's Kingdom was a reality, yet, at the same time, unthreatening to the power alignment that existed between Jewish leaders and the Roman Army. Otherwise, the leaders would rush in to protect their privileged and profitable arrangement with the Romans (cf. Jn. 11:48-50). Second, Jesus had to proclaim the Kingdom in terms that would not mislead the common people into expecting a utopia in which they would no longer be powerless before the outside world. Yet Jesus promised that His followers would not remain powerless in the world. They would indeed receive power but it would be for a different purpose: to be His witnesses unto the uttermost parts of the earth (Acts 1:8).

On religious fervor and the bandit mystique. The common people of first century Palestine were known for their religious fervor and expectations of a Messiah. Their concept of the Messiah, however, resembled more the bandit mystique found in peasant society than what was revealed in the Scriptures. On one occasion, after feeding the 5000, the people in their fervor wanted to make Jesus King (Jn. 6:15). But Jesus withdrew, refusing to be properly proclaimed King. Even during His triumphant entry into Jerusalem (Jn. 12:12-19), Jesus refused to fulfill the people's expectations for a popular Messiah, for while he commended the people's fervor His purpose in accepting it was not to lead them in a revolution or to overthrow the power structure. His purpose was to show that the Messiah, as well as God's Kingdom, was "not of this world", an aspect of the Messiahship that the disciples did not grasp until Jesus' glorification (Jn. 12:16).

In summary: In proclaiming the Good News of the Kingdom in first century Palestine, Jesus sought to change the culture of Jewish peasant society (the social significance of this observation will be discussed below). Cultural traits, such as excessive ceremonialism, distrust, feelings of powerlessness, religious fervor and the bandit mystique, were to be corrected in the light of Jesus' teachings and example. In place of these traits there were to emerge new personality traits in those individuals who accepted the Good News as proclaimed by Jesus Christ. In place of ceremonialism there was to be concern (cf. "It is lawful no the sabbath to do good or to do harm?" Mk. 2:4). Trust was to replace distrust (cf. "leave your gift there at the altar . . . and be reconciled with your brother" Mt. 5:24). Religious fervor was to be properly channeled (cf. "This is the work of God, that you believe in him whom he has sent" Jn. 6:29). And, of course, the bandit mystique had to be laid to rest permanently in the light that God's Kingdom is not of this world. Even an attachment to Palestine as the Promised Land was to be replaced by something far greater (cf. "behold, something greater than Solomon is here" Lk. 11:31).

The same results must be the outcome of communicating the Gospel in peasant society today. It is peasant cultural life that must be transformed by the message of the Gospel. In place of the old cultural traits, a new command must be inaugurated: "that you love one another, even as I have loved you" (Jn. 13:34). The old cultural traits, the product of the way peasant society is organized, are to be transformed into the new life in Jesus Christ. Old personality traits, long tied in to the peasant cultural situation, are to be changed to the likeness of Jesus Christ Himself.

SOCIAL REVOLUTION: A VALID EVANGELISTIC GOAL IN PEASANT SOCIETY?

Peasant societies (since they contain half of the world's population) have come under the attention of theologians. This attention has come from two directions. First, it has come from the ecumenical movement, especially in the movement's emphasis on the humanization of social structures (Peter Beyerhaus 1971). Society, in its organizational structure, is to be made more humane for humans; inequalities in terms of power, for example, are to be alleviated if not eliminated altogether. Humanization, therefore, functions as a type of *pre-evangelization*, preparing the sociological ground for a later reaping of the harvest and the establishment of the church in society. A second and more recent direction for the attention paid to the world's peasant societies has been liberation theology and its emphasis upon the analysis of *why* there are socially oppressed groups and what can be done so these groups can achieve their share of power in the world. This attention from liberation theology has even more recently been extended to include the rural masses who have fled to the urban centers of the world and are now powerless in their new environment. In their attention to the powerless groups of today's world, both the ecumenical movement and liberation theology tend to be quite radical in analyzing and providing solutions to social problems. The solution proposed is liberation from social injustices and inequality, a solution that may involve social revolution in the name of God.

The ecumenical movement is the older of the two, being built on 19th century and early 20th century liberalism. It was a philosophy optimistic both in its assessment of the human condition and its prediction of where the human race was heading. Unfortunately, though, World War I, the rise of Hitler and Stalin, World War II and the atomic bomb destroyed optimism as a valid assessment of the human condition. Along with optimism, liberalism also died.

Because of its liberal and optimistic view of man, the ecumenical movement suffered from an inherent weakness in communicating the (liberal version of the) Gospel in the world. While the ecumenical movement had a hermeneutic (in the form of liberal theology) for understanding and interpreting the Bible, it had no comparable hermeneutic for accurately understanding the world other than a vague evolutionary scheme of mankind progressing toward the Kingdom of God. As it turned out, liberalism and optimism were not relevant to the world of Auschwitz, Siberian labor camps and Hiroshima. Even after liberalism was dead, the picture did not appreciably change, for in place of liberalism came neo-orthodoxy, which again was primarily a biblical hermeneutic and only secondarily a social hermeneutic for understanding the world. The effect was the same: neo-orthodoxy was ill-equipped as a hermeneutic for understanding a world that was now divided into the powerful and powerless, the oppressor and oppressed, and the dominate and dominated, etc. To fill this void the ecumenical movement turned to liberation theology.

Liberation theology is largely a Latin American and Roman Catholic formulation (Jose Miquez Bonino 1975), although Protestants have also contributed to its development. But while it is a theology, it also goes beyond traditional theology in two significant ways. First, it is a *social hermeneutic* for analyzing and understanding the world, and, second, it offers solutions by the very nature of the social problems it reveals, i.e., the solutions for social problems revealed by the hermeneutic are derived from and based upon the analysis. This is an aspect that gives liberation theology a strong revolutionary flavor. Now if liberation theology were only a social hermeneutic, it would perhaps amount to little more than a moderate critique of current social conditions. But being "moderate" in liberation theology is difficult, if not impossible, because of the particular social hermeneutic chosen, for in choosing this hermeneutic it is difficult to escape the solutions inherent in the analysis.

The social hermeneutic adopted by liberation theology is a modified Marxism. Karl Marx (1883-1881), in his analysis of society, focused upon economics as the determinative factor that controls and shapes social life. Not only is social life shaped by economics, Marx alleged, but man himself is molded and shaped by the way society is organized economically. From this emphasis Marx accurately predicted that economics would become the most important social institution in the modern world. No less accurate was his analysis that the mode of production (as an aspect of economics) determines the class structure of society, viz., society becomes divided into the exploiters and the exploited. The exploiters, according to Marx, are the bourgeoisie, the owners of the capital resources of society and who, by virtue of their wealth, control the means of production. The exploited are the proletariat (working class) who have only their labor and brute strength to sell to the capitalists. Drawing upon the dialectic method of Georg Wilhelm Friedrich Hegel (1770-1832), a German philospher, Marx saw in the capitalists the "thesis" with proletariat forming the "antithesis." Less accurately, however, was his forecast that the two sides would inevitably clash, and out of the struggle would come a "synthesis", viz., socialism, where the proletariat would take over ownership of production and thus be in control of their own destiny.

Marx also saw in this struggle a *materialistic* explanation for the progression of history. History is not being directed by God, Marx claimed, nor is history advancing to a consummation of the ages when God shall once again reign over His creation. In fact, God does not exist; there is only matter, or "material", in interaction. It is this materialistic aspect of Marxism that is rejected in liberation theology. Other aspects, of course, are accepted.

> For some of us Marxism can be assumed at this level. It is an analysis of the way in which socio-economic-political reality functioned at a certain point in history (the stage of capitalism which Marx observed). This analysis was significantly projected into an hypothesis concerning the relation of human history . . . to the process of producing material goods. As an hypothesis it has been tested against our knowledge of the past and against conditions obtaining late on and in different situations. It has been refined, supplemented, or developed. But it seems to many of us that it has proved, and still proves to be, the best instrument available for an effective and rational realization of human possibilities in historical life. A Marxist praxis is both the verification and the source of possible corrections of the hypothesis (Jose Miguez Bonino 1975:97).

There is another significant modification to Marxism that has been made in liberation theology, a modification, perhaps, that Marx could not foresee. Marx was concerned with formulating a theory that would predict the various stages that individual societies must pass through in order to become classless, socialist societies. When an individual society had passed through all the stages and had become a classless society, there would be, among other things, no government; in fact, there would be no need for government, as every human need would be fulfilled by the socialist method of production and distribution of goods. Presumably, therefore—although this is not quite explicit in Marx—as each individual society becomes class-less and socialist, all governments would disappear, and the world's societies would merge into one society where each one would be producing according to ability and each one receiving goods and services according to need.

What Marx did not foresee, but which liberation theology has added, is this: just as an individual society is divided into an exploit-ing class and an exploited class, so is the world divided into exploit-ing societies and exploited societies. Marx, in other words, because he lived too early in history, could focus only on the *microsociologi-cal level*, while liberation theology, because of more recent world developments, can extend his analysis to the *macrosociological level*. In many respects this extension is not unlike the thesis underlying this book. Just as we have claimed that relationships among social institutions in a society (microsociology) are important parameters in evangelism, so does liberation theology claim that relationships among types of societies (macrosociology) are equally important parameters in communicating the Gospel in today's world. Societies are divided into different types in liberation theology than what has been done in this book. In liberation theology a society, or nation, is classified as either an exploiting society (e.g., the industrial nations of the northern hemisphere) or an exploited society (e.g., the nations of the Third World).

This extension of Marxism has been the basis for the liberation theology's critique of international aid from the industrial countries to Third World nations (Gustave Gutierrez 1973). The purpose of international aid programs has been to aid in the development of underdeveloped Third World societies; it is, in effect, a voluntary redistribution of wealth on an international level. However, as it has turned out according to the Marxist analysis made in liberation theology, it has not been a true redistribution. Rather, a "sociology of redistribution" has been in effect, i.e., wealth is redistributed in order to maintain, if not actually increase, the social and economic dependency of Third World nations to the industrial nations. Nothing is really gained by giving aid if in the end the gift makes the receiver dependent upon the giver.

Even western style socialism comes under the same critique. Wealth under a socialist government is redistributed, but the exploit-ing class, the capitalists, even though less wealthy because of exten-sive taxation, still survives and consequently has the greater power in society. The only solution for such persistent social problems is the *liberation* from dependency on the part of Third World societies, as well as *liberation* from powerlessness on the part of oppressed groups in society. Such liberation may indeed involve a radical social revolution, the overthrow of the existing social order (whether on a macro- or microsociological level), for a more liberated order that embodies the ideals of justice found in the Kingdom of God. At this point theology, now in its more traditional meaning of a "scientific" study of the nature of God's Kingdom, is used to support the liberation theme of a Marxist analysis of society and the world.

Obviously, liberation theology differs radically from our approach to cross-cultural communication, even though both share the same beginning point, social organization, in the task of communicating the Gospel cross-culturally. The difference, however, lies in the utilization of this starting point. For liberation theology (including now the ecumenical movement), social organization (especially the structural dimension of how society is organized) becomes the object of change and not merely an interpretive device for understanding the context wherein the Gospel is to be proclaimed. Communicating the Gospel is not, as advocated in the outset of this book, to achieve the goal of correctly understanding the content of the Gospel so individual members of society may be persuaded to believe on Jesus Christ. Social revolution—an ideological position becoming more popular in liberation theology—is the goal of communicating the Gospel among oppressed peoples in today's world.

This difference aside, however, our basic question remains. Is social revolution a valid goal in the missionary task of communicating the Gospel cross-culturally in oppressed societies? Obviously, when compared to the communicative goals of understanding and persuasion established at the outset of this book, social revolution is not valid. But beyond this lack of "fit", there are three, more fundamental reasons why social revolution is not valid.

First, Marxism as the social hermeneutic of choice in liberation theology—a hermeneutic that leads to social revolution as the fuction of its application in oppressed situations—is an arbitrary selection. Liberation theology, at this point, could just as arbitrarily, and with just as much justification, have chosen the sociological model of structure-function, with its emphasis on maintaining the status quo, as its social hermeneutic! There is no *a priori* reason for choosing Marxism over structure-function or any other model available in the sociological market place. Of course, if some other model had been chosen, the resulting communicative goals in liberation theology would have been different. But arbitrariness does not stop at the selection of Marxism as the social hermeneutic in liberation theology. There is also no *a priori* reason for focusing upon the interpretation of social organization as the first task of the missionary in communicating the Gospel in the world. But even if social interpretation should be the first task, it still would not follow that Marxism should be the hermeneutical framework. Because of this arbitrariness, doubt is also cast, both on liberation from social oppression as the *content* of the Gospel; and on mission strategy which encompasses the support of terrorist groups fighting to overthrow repressive governments.

By way of contrast, consider the choice of structure-function as a basic component in our model for communicating the Gospel. By this choice, we escape the arbitrariness above because social structure (more precisely, social organization) is not the object of analysis. Rather, culture is the object of analysis and interpretation. The way society is organized, then, becomes the logical beginning point in understanding culture. At this point it also follows logically that the content of the Gospel is something different than social revolution and that strategy of communication encompasses the task of making the Gospel relevant to the social context, i.e., so that the Gospel's content "speaks" in judgment over the particular social relationships existing in society. Therefore, if cultural hermeneutics is based on social organization, then social hermeneutics would have to based on something else, a process, unfortunately, that remains frustratingly unresolvable—unless, of course, an ideology such as Marxism is arbitrarily chosen!

The second reason why social revolution is not a valid goal in communicating the Gospel stems from the nature of the Marxist dialectic. By accepting Marxism, liberation theology has, in effect, stated that the Gospel functions as the "antithesis" to social conditions currently found in today's world. Now this function for the Gospel in the world is scriptural, but at this point the Marxist dialectic breaks down as a social hermeneutic for liberation theology. The dialectic method states that in the struggle between the thesis (+ current social conditions) and the antithesis (+ the Gospel), there will emerge a synthesis. Liberation theology predicts that this synthesis will be a new liberated world order, an order where individuals will be liberated from current social conditions of oppression and powerlessness. Such an analysis of the future, however, even though required by the dialectic method of Marxism, is not supported by the Scriptures. According to the Scriptures, the ultimate end in the struggle between the Gospel and the world is not a synthesis of the two but the victory of the former over the latter: "The kingdom of this world has become the kingdom of our Lord and of his Christ, and He shall reign for ever and ever" (Rev. 11:15). The Scriptures predict that the "earth and the works that are upon it will be burned up" (2 Pet. 3:10). Our goal as missionary communicators of the Gospel, therefore, should not be achieving a new synthesis between the world and the Gospel but the preparation of individuals through the proclamation of the Gospel for the final victory.

The third reason why social revolution is rejected as a valid goal in communicating the Good News of the Kingdom is the example of Jesus. In the previous section we noted that Jewish society of First Century Palestine contained several repressive elements, e.g., an elite in the form of the Pharisees and scribes, the Roman occupational forces, etc. We also observed that Jesus sought to change not the social situation but culture—the values, beliefs, norms, personality traits, etc.—of those who followed Him. If the example of Jesus means anything in the task of communicating His Gospel in today's world, it means that the product of this task is cultural change. Along this same line there is perhaps a divine wisdom in the statement "The poor you always have with you" (Jn. 12:9) that heretofore has escaped us. If the poor are also the powerless of society, then Jesus' statement also means there will always be oppression in society. As heartless as this may sound, it is unfortunately still provable in just those societies that claim to have eliminated oppression, viz., the Marxist and communist societies of today. In such cases the Marxist or communist elite have become the new oppressors while the non-marxists and noncommunists have become the oppressed. And if there is any lesson for liberation theology to be gained from contemporary Marxist societies, it is this: the same will turn out to be true for any future "liberated" society, because being based on Marxism, there will arise a Marxist, or "liberated", elite to subjugate and oppress those who, in the process, must assume the status of common people in society. Therefore, if there is any "humanization" through proclamation of the Gospel, it is to be accomplished through the creation of a new "humane culture" in the midst of society.

THE CHURCH: GOD'S REVOLUTIONARY KINGDOM IN SOCIETY

Having stated above our commitment against social revolution as a valid goal in communicating the Gospel in today's world, we must hasten to balance the picture lest it be misunderstood that humanization has no part in the Kingdom. Christians, after all, are God's "workmanship, created in Christ Jesus for good works, which God prepared beforehand, that we should walk with them" (Eph. 2:10). One good work is "to do good to all men" (Gal. 6:10): to feed the hungry, to give water to the thirsty, to welcome strangers, to clothe the naked, to visit the sick and those in prison (Mt. 25:35-40). To neglect these good works is to be cursed, condemned to the eternal fire prepared for the devil and his angels (Mt. 24:41). These good works, furthermore, must function as a judgment upon society: "You are the salt of the earth" (Mt. 5:13). Without the example of good works from Christians, society would indeed become a harsh environment. The influence of good works, therefore, must feed into society, transforming culture so that society may become more humane. "Let your light so shine before men, that they may see your good works and give glory to your father who is in heaven" (Mt. 5:16).

While humanization is a theme in the New Testament, it is not the major thrust of the Gospel. The major thrust is the creation of a new revolutionary social unit in the midst of (fallen) society. In fact, there is a certain pessimism in the New Testament about society being capable of reformation. On the other hand, there is no pessimism regarding the reformation of the individual nor regarding the gathering of reformed individuals into a separate, revolutionary kingdom. The revolutionary nature of the kingdom can be seen in the fact that within it "there is neither Jew nor Greek . . . neither slave or free . . . neither male or female" (Gal. 3:28), and greatness measured in terms of service and not in terms of status (Mt. 23:11). And the less honorable members of the Kingdom are to receive the greater honor.

Jesus Himself established the prototype of the new Kingdom in choosing His band of twelve disciples. He called both a Zealot (in behalf of Palestine as a geographical area belonging only to the Jews) and a tax collector (for the Roman occupiers of Palestine). He also called Peter (who evidently preferred his Jewish names of Simon and Cephas) and Philip (who evidently preferred his Hellenistic name over whatever Jewish name he may have had). Jesus welded these and others together into a new social unit based, not on the political categories of the day (e.g., Essene, Pharisee, Sadducee, etc.), but on a new commandment that transcended these categories, and forging, in effect, not only a new Kingdom but also a new culture or way of life.

The church of God's revolutionary Kingdom on earth is the fulfillment of any Marxist or liberated ideals regarding just societies. In fact, as Francis Schaeffer (1976) claims, Marxism in its idealism should be regarded as little more than a heretical form of Christianity. Marxism, for example, recognizes that history is meaningful and is progressing to an end; however, the meaning behind history is not God but a blind dialectic, and the end toward which history is heading is not the reign of God over His creation, but a socialism where all things material and economic will be equally shared.

Even though the Church is the fulfillment of the ideals in Marxism and liberation theology, we must admit that in practice the Church has more often than not failed in this regard: the main criticism that can be leveled against the Church is that she has not lived up to her revolutionary expectations in society. The Church has often been merely a reflection and supporter of the way society is organized instead of reflecting the true nature of God's Kingdom. All too often in the world's history the Church has only reinforced prevailing governmental and economic structures, structures moreover that favor the elite and powerful over the powerless in society. Even worse, the same social divisions have often been instituted in the Church herself, a condition that came under the severe condemnation of James, the Lord's brother (James 2:1-7).

To sum up: In proclaiming the Gospel in peasant societies, and in oppressed societies in general, the missionary communicator must proclaim the ramifications of the Gospel regarding liberation from oppression and domination as fulfilled in the Church. The Church constitutes, in other words, the "sociological package" wherein the content of the Gospel is wrapped for communication in peasant society. But the Church accomplishes more than becoming a liberated social unit in the midst of oppression. The Church also becomes the area where culture is changed, i.e., where the old cultural and personality traits are transformed and the new man (even the new man of Marxist ideology) emerges. The results, as the Apostle Paul wrote, are radical and revolutionary. "From now, therefore, we regard no one from a human point of view; even though we once regarded Christ from a human point of view. Therefore, if any one is in Christ, he is a new creation; the old has passed away, behold the new has come" (2 Cor. 5:16-17).

Chapter 8
Communicating The Gospel
In Modern Society

Danay was the only student to show up for my class on sociology of religion that day. Both he and I had missed the announcement that the day had been declared "skip day" for Chiang Mai University, the university of the northern area of Thailand. Since there was nothing else to do, we sat in the classroom and talked. Danay soon turned the conversation to a topic that was bothering him. "*Acharn*", he addressed me in the Thai equivalent of professor, "How can we eliminate corruption in our government?"

I was stumped for a moment over how to answer Danay's question, but I did manage to answer in the only way I knew how. When I did answer it was Danay's turn to be stumped. "There is really only one way to eliminate corruption" I replied, "and that is by conversion to Jesus Christ." Danay expressed his puzzlement as to how conversion or even religion could help in such a crucial matter. I tried to explain, but our conversation quickly turned to such basic matters as the existence of God, how do we know He exists, what are the proofs of His existence, and so on.

A few days later some students in Bangkok were arrested for distributing leaflets calling for a return to constitutional government. The arrest, however, resulted in radicalizing the students of Thailand, including Danay. So in a second conversation on government and corruption, Danay began to discuss the need to arrest the generals who are in control of the military government and punish if not execute them. I emphasized again conversion as the cure for corruption, but I also hastened to emphasize that God is the final judge and avenger. I explained that God is no respector of persons but will judge both the great and small in the last judgment. My proclamation of the judgment must have caught Danay's imagination because he immediately asked "When will God do this?" Realizing he was interested mainly in revenge I hastened again to explain that God at the present was more interested in giving all men more opportunity to repent (2 Pet. 3:9). Unfortunately, to Danay's thinking, now radicalized by the arrests of fellow students, repentance was too slow as a means for correcting the current corrupt situation.

Because of the students' arrest, Danay became a political activist, and during the student-led revolt of October, 1973, he led a group of high school and university students in occupying the Chiang Mai provincial capital building. During the uprising, which was nationwide and had widespread popular support, a picture of Danay, appeared in a national newspaper; he was standing on the capital's steps and addressing the crowd of students through a megaphone. Underneath the picture was a short description of his role in organizing and leading the Chiang Mai secton of the revolt. I must admit I felt a tinge of pride when I showed Danay's picture to my wife announcing that he was one of my students!

Danay was a brilliant student; a teaching position had already been promised him at the university after he graduated with his second B.A. degree. More significantly, though, was the cognitive map he used for making sense of the world: even in a land where animism is widely practiced and 80% of the population are peasants, his strategy for organizing the world about him was thoroughly modern. His major concern was no longer religion or the land, but government and economics, especially when the two are combined for the profit of the government bureaucrat. So while his father was a Buddhist and his mother Christian, he was neither. In short, Danay demonstrated in his life and thinking those fundamental shifts so characteristic of modern society, viz., the load for maintaining society that at one time was assigned to religion and family had shifted to the social institutions of government and economics.

This chapter explores the nature of modern society and what strategies may be used in communicating the Gospel to modern individuals. Since we saw in the previous chapter that the Kingdom was first proclaimed under peasant circumstances, we may wonder what potential there is in the Scriptures for proclaiming the Kingdom in modern society. The question is especially pertinent since, under our framework and definition of social change, religion no longer performs significant societal functions in maintaining society. Yet, in spite of this development, we shall see that the Gospel is indeed relevant for modern society. To accomplish this, however, we first need a characterization both of modern society and the role that religion as a social institution performs in forming the cognitive map that individuals in modern society use in organizing the world.

MODERN SOCIETY: A CHARACTERIZATION

Modern society is much more complex than either tribal or peasant society. In reality modern society is too complex to adequately characterize in the brief space allowed in this section. Yet, because the Great Commission was meant to include modern society along with other types of societies, we must make such an attempt, at least an attempt to characterize those features relevant for communicating the Gospel cross-culturally in modern society.

One complexity characteristic of modern society is that it no longer forms a homogeneous type as compared to either tribal or peasant society. Sociologists now speak of two (sub)types of modern society, industrial society and post-industrial society. While both share many features in common they still differ in important details that, in the end, affect the communication of the Gospel. To adequately characterize modern society, we must describe both.

Industrial society is the older of the two subtypes; it is also the stage into which the more recent modern societies have entered. The most common feature of industrial society is industrialization, more precisely the industrialization of the means of producing goods. The industrial era of human history began in the latter part of the 18th century in England. New inventions in manufacturing, transportation, and in harnessing energy began the era, and it was not long before these inventions had spread to the rest of Europe and America. Industrialization brought about several rapid changes in the way society was organized. One such change was the shift in population from rural areas to urban areas where the industries were located. This shift, in time, turned society into *mass society*, where large numbers of people lived in a relatively small land area. The rise of both industrialization and the concentration of large numbers of people created new strains on government. To cope with such changes and to meet the new challenges of mass society, government *bureaucracies* were established. Yet even with bureaucracies to keep society functioning, strains within mass society persisted, strains which created in their wake a way of living vastly different from rural life. As families were formed and children were born in the new urban environment, new patterns of socialization emerged. While these new patterns had the more immediate function of turning children into acceptable members of mass society, they also were creating a new and different cognitive map for selecting data from the world and organizing the data into new systems of knowledge. In sum, industrialization created a new type of culture distinct from both tribal and peasant culture.

The effects of industrialization, as just described, is also called modernization, i.e., the cognitive map that a society offers to its members for making sense of the world is modern and not tribal or peasant in character. More specifically in our terms, a modern cognitive map states that all knowledge is not interrelated or holistic as in tribal society but is compartmentalized into various autonomous areas. Furthermore, religion, as an area of knowledge, is not necessary or important as in peasant society. The former development results in specialization, while the latter results in secularization. When the cognitive map of a society results in autonomous areas of knowledge (specialization) and secularization, society is said to be modern.

Modernization, however, is much more pervasive than what the preceding paragraph indicates. Donald Light, Jr. and Suzanne Keller (1975), for example, cite three major transformations in the way society is organized under the impact of modernization. The first is called *political modernization*, where functions formerly carried by religion and family are now consolidated in the state, more specifically in a centralized state bureaucracy. One result of this is that the state or government no longer seeks legitimation for its existence from divine sources; rather, legitimation now comes from ideology and political parties. The second major transformation is called *social modernization*, where, in addition to intensive urbanization, large commercial and communication enterprises emerge. To provide skilled personnel for such organizations educational and literacy programs are instituted. As a result, social mobility emerges as a dynamic of social life, and in the end there is a change away from local and ethnic allegiance to organizational and class allegiance. The third major transformation that occurs as a society becomes modern is called *psychological modernization*. In this transformation individuals become change-oriented as well as future-oriented, and there emerges an abiding faith that man can truly dominate nature and thereby make planned changes in the way nature operates.

Psychological modernization results into what Max Weber (1864-1920) termed *rationalization*. Because people in modern society are oriented to planning for change, modern culture assumes an aura of calculation and manipulation. People in modern society become "disenchanted" with the way things are, and so they calculate alternate schemes for creating a better social environment. Such calculations, as Phillip E. Hammon et al (1975) state, give rise to three broad developments in modern society. The first is greater specialization of function, i.e., the means of achieving goals in society are narrowed into highly specific tasks. Two examples of this narrowing effect are found in the social institutions of family and religion. Both become organized into smaller units to perform fewer functions in society. Yet, functions formerly filled by these two institutions must still be fulfilled. Consequently, there comes, as a second development of rationalization, a proliferation of organizations to fulfill these functions. As family and religion cease to be moral forces in society, police and judicial organizations are created to enforce the moral

order of society. As more organizations are created, each one performing a more narrow range of functions, they become highly
interdependent. Such interdependency is the third development of
rationalization. Modern society, in short, is conceived in terms of a
highly complex but well organized machine where each component
performs its specialized task in tandem with all other components.

Complexity in social organization is not without its cost. The
narrowing in functional role of key social institutions as the family
and religion has extracted its toll on modern society. While there are
newly created organizations to make sure all essential functions are
fulfilled, it is an open question whether these organizations can, in
the end, perform them as well as the traditional institutions. But
given the "forward" direction that rationalization takes, a return to
traditional institutions, as a means of fulfilling these functions, is not
considered. Rather, more organizations and bureaucratic structures
are created in order to make up what is still lacking in the older
bureaucratic organizations. Unfortunately, such proliferation of
organizations results in increased social fragmentation and in the end
society ceases to function as a well-organized machine.

To add to the above complexity is the emergence of post-industrial
society in today's world. The term post-industrial society was first
coined by Daniel Bell (1973) to describe a detectable shift observable
in American society and which undoubtedly—assuming all other
things are equal—will occur in other industrial countries. According
to Bell, the chief economic problem in an industrial society is capital,
more precisely, how to institutionalize a process for accumulating
and investing money in order to produce goods. In capitalist economies, this process has taken the form of banks, stock markets and
self-financing. In socialist economies, the process has included
extensive taxation and the investment of tax monies in heavy industry. In the shift to post-industrial society, however, the chief problem
is the organization of science and knowledge. The primary institutions for such organization are the university and research laboratory. Whereas in industrial society strength lies in productive capacity, the strength of post-industrial society is the harnessing of
knowledge.

This change in the way the modern society is organized, Daniel
Bell claimed, ramifies throughout all of society. Specifically, Bell
spells out four main areas which the change to post-industrial society
affects.

Creation of a service economy. Production declines in the shift to
post-industrial society, and in its place there emerges an emphasis on
service occupations. As the change to post-industrial society acceler-
ates, the economy assumes a different character: jobs in the factory

and on the assembly line decrease, but openings in the professional and service sector of the economy increase. After a certain point, modern society becomes consumer-oriented. Unfortunately, at this stage, inflation becomes a major problem as less goods are now produced but consumption is greater, thus creating greater demand for the fewer goods that are produced. This pushes prices even higher. Inflation is further aggravated by the fact that consumer services are not easily amendable to production increases, since a person who is providing a service can physically provide only so much personal service in the time limitation of an eight-hour working day. Yet in order not to fall behind in living standards, because of such limitations, people in service occupations demand wage increases to keep pace with the inflation caused by fewer goods being produced.

Experts assume a greater role in managing society. The main task in post-industrial society is organizing knowledge. This task requires experts, people who themselves are highly trained and skilled in the various areas of science and specialized knowledge needed to keep society functioning. This enlarged role of experts in turn strengthens the role of science and cognitive values in society. Because knowledge is now so technical, experts assume a greater role in the political process and decision-making in society. As experts and their specialized, technical knowledge become indispensable in maintaining society, those versed in the literary traditions become less important, if not expendable, in the social system.

Theoretical knowledge becomes central in innovating change and formulating policy. Knowledge has always been important for maintaining any type of society, but in post-industrial society, it is not knowledge in an ordinary sense that is essential. It is theoretical knowledge that is central to the maintenance of society. Empirical and "how-to" knowledge become secondary in importance, and in its place, theory, or model-making—the codification of knowledge into abstract systems of symbols—becomes primary. For example, the methods of accumulating capital for investments, a prime concern in industrial society, is replaced by the need to construct overarching theoretical models of economics so that the complexity and fragmentation of post-industrial society, now more consumer- oriented than production-oriented, can be more smoothly integrated.

Technology becomes pre-eminent in society. In fact, technology becomes autonomous and self-innovating, i.e., new technologies are created simply because it is possible to do so. Obviously, this feeds into and reinforces the consumerism of post-industrial society: new technology, after all, must also be financed. Hence, sophisticated marketing techniques are designed to sell the new technological innovations to an ever consumer-conscious society. At this point the circle is completed only to start over again on a more intense cycle of post-industrialization and the "consumerization" of society.

While the post-industrial society is still a new and imperfectly understood development in today's world, one fact appears clear as based on what has occurred in American society: inflation, because of the emphasis on service occupations and consumerism, becomes a serious problem that threatens the maintenance of society. As a result, in order to keep society functioning, it has recently been recommended that America be "reindustrialized." A reindustrialization of society would involve a reversal of a service-and consumer-oriented economy and a reemphasis on industrialization, i.e., the accumulation of capital for investment in industry. Economically, a good case can be made for the reindustrialization of America. America's industrial plants are for the most part old and inefficient. Their rate of production or output is slow as compared to the industries of other industrial nations; even if American industry wanted to produce more (thereby lowering the price of each unit produced), very little could be accomplished along this line because of outdated technology. To correct this, it is recommended that American industry be rebuilt with new and more efficient technologies, for only in this way can the prices of goods decrease and the inflation of post-industrial society be brought under control.

If the reindustrialization of American society is successful, what will be the changes that will follow in the way American society is organized? Will post-industrialism, with its emphasis on consumerism, be truly reversed? Will the role of experts in education, government, etc. decrease? Will theoretical knowledge decrease in importance and "Yankee ingenuity" once again become supreme in society? It is obviously too early to tell. But whatever the outcome it will be a factor that must be taken into account in communicating the Gospel in American society.

RELIGION IN MODERN SOCIETY

In Chapter V we characterized religion in modern society with the following features:

[-holistic + compartmentalized - important]

These features are meant to characterize only the relationship (hence the functions) that religion has as a social institution vis-a-vis the other social institution in the maintenance of modern society. As these features show, religion has little, if any, functional interdependency with the other social institutions in maintaining modern society. For example, religion is [- holistic], i.e., there is no necessary *religious* dimension in the functioning of government, economics, education and family in the way modern society is organized. Rather, religion is compartmentalized into its own autonomous area of society. Finally, religion is [- important], i.e., as a social institution religion is not crucial for the maintenance of modern society.

Cognitively [- important] plays a highly significant role in the way modern society is perceived to be organized. It forms an integral part of the cognitive map that individuals in modern society use in making sense of today's world. As part of the modern cognitive map, religion as [- important] carries the same amount of information or impact as religion, characterized as [+ important], does in tribal society; the feature [- important] plays just as *positive* a role in the way modern society is organized with respect to religion as [+ important] does for tribal society. The feature [- important] is also an essential component in the cognitive strategy upon which individuals in modern society make decisions. Religion, for instance, is to play no important role in making economic, governmental or educational decisions, nor should it be a dominant factor in choosing a spouse, socializing children, and in taking care of the elderly in society. In short, the feature [- important] forms an 'essential part of the total sociological base in modern society upon which communications are encoded, transmitted and interpreted.

Of the three features that characterize religion in modern society, the feature [- important] is the most significant for our purposes. It is significant because as a feature it stands for a complex set of religious trends and counter-trends that in turn makes religion in modern society as complex as modern society itself. Figure 7 below summarizes for us these trends and counter trends. But before proceeding to a detailed discussion of the trends and counter-trends represented in Figure 7, four general observations about the diagram should be made.

First, the basic division between secularization and individualism is meant to show that religion, even as [- important], does not necessarily disappear from modern society. On the contrary, as religion decreases as a social value in modern society, it may increase as an individual value; this process has several significant ramifications for communicating the Gospel in modern society. Second, secularization is here considered essentially a religious phenomenon in modern society. This is based on the analogy of negative numbers in mathematics: just as negative numbers are as real as positive numbers, so is secularization (here equal to [- religion] in society) just as real in terms of (negative) religious impact as [+ religion] is in more traditional societies. Third, the above diagram does not represent stages that everyone in modern society must go through. Of course,

Religion as [- important]

Secularization

Individualistic

Functional Shift

Religion as Subjectivism

Narrowing of Role

Instrumental Religion

Emphasis on self-fulfillment
and not on self-denial for
service

Subsitute Religion

Emphasis on materialism
and / or ideology

"Post-industrial Religion"

"Consumer-oriented religion"

Cults

Rejection of materialism, (secular) ideology
and the individualism of post-industrial religion
for a more "group conscious" religion

Figure 7

many individuals do pass through these stages and end up as members of cults. Many others, though, stop along the way, remaining at one stage or another for the rest of their lives. Fourth, the above diagram in its totality is also meant to show the mosaic that religion is in modern society. A characteristic of modern society is pluralism whether in life style, ethnic composition, marriage and family arrangements, occupations, etc. Religion in modern society is no less pluralistic, whether in terms of different beliefs or in its various sociological manifestations.

Figure 7 shows two paths that religion in modern society may take. One is secularization which is a societal phenomenon, and the other is individualism, where religion becomes an individual and private matter. Either path may end up at the same place, cultism, but more of this below. Each path sets in motion certain trends for religious behavior in modern society.

First, under secularization, we see three trends for religion in modern society. In fact, it is these trends that give secularization its definition as a religious phenomenon of modern society.

Functional Shift. In secularization the first trend is for functions that are normally fulfilled by religion to shift away from religion to become fulfilled by other social institutions. In Chapter 2, for example, we saw where religion performs three major functions in society: religion defines the nature of transcendance, the historical destiny of society, and establishes for society what questions in life are ultimate as well as what the answers to these questions should be. But in modern society these functions have shifted away from religion and have become associated with other social institutions, most notably government and education. Government now defines what the destiny of society is, education establishes those questions that should be ultimate as well as the framework for their answers.

Narrowing of Role. As functions shift away to be fulfilled by other social institutions, religion undergoes a second trend, narrowing of role in society; there is little left for religion to do in maintaining society. On the other hand, it is this narrowing of role that increases the institutionalization of religion in modern society. As its societal role decreases, a counter-trend sets in: religion as a social institution becomes more compartmentalized, hence more highly visible in society. As religion becomes institutionalized, it becomes more autonomous from other social institutions, having its own corps of specialists whose main role is more for the maintenance of the institution than for the maintenance of society. It is, as though for survival's sake, religion in modern society becomes more prominent in order to offset the decrease in societal importance that results from secularization.

Substitute Religion. Defining the nature of transcendence, the historical destiny of the group and what are ultimate questions, however, are essentially religious functions, even though in modern society they become associated with other social institutions. At this point we must remember that religion is still a basic institution even in modern society. Similarly, the functions just mentioned are basically religious in nature, even though they are performed by other social institutions in modern society. Consequently, when these functions are separated from religion, a void in social life occurs: on the one hand traditional beliefs are dead or no longer socially viable, but on the other neither government nor education can adequately perform these functions for society. To fill this void, substitute religions are created. The most common substitute that individuals in modern society create to replace traditional belief is materialism. The best known example of this is the "civil religion" of U.S. society. The American way of life (pluralism, economic growth, etc.) has become a substitute for the Judeo-Christian tradition of an earlier age. Other common substitutes for religion in modern society include ideology (e.g., Marxism, fascism, etc.), political activism, and even patriotism.

The second path in Figure 7 on page 140, and which religion may take in modern society, is individualism. Actually, individualism is a counter-trend to secularization. Secularization, which is largely a product of western societies, had its beginnings in the west before the Protestant Reformation. In fact, it was an important underlying cause of the Reformation. The Reformation, in turn, allowed the secularization process to increase and have its full effect in society. By the 19th century numerous scholars (e.g., Karl Marx, Auguste Comte) were predicting the disappearance of religion from the face of the earth. What these scholars failed to anticipate, however, was the counter-trend that religion would take in modern, secular society. As religion decreases in social importance it would increase in individual importance. Far from disappearing from the earth, religion has survived and has even gained ground in modern society as an individual and private matter.

As counter-trend to secularization, individualism in religion sets in motion certain trends of its own. These trends, as shown in Figure 7, stand as counter-parts to those listed under secularization.

Religion as Subjectivism. With religion stripped of its importance for defining and regulating the social relationships existing among members of society, there remains only the personal, subjective world of the individual where religion may still be important. The early Protestant Reformers grasped the significance of this sociological process. John Calvin, for example, proclaimed that one can be saved only by subjectively knowing God. This subjectivism stood in opposition to one's knowledge about God which may be considerable but which has no power to save. Later Soren Kierkegaard, in order to preserve religious belief in an era of advancing secularization, introduced existentialism and his "leap of faith", a theology that drew upon subjectivism to provide a foundation for the survival of Christianity in western society. Today subjectivism is still foundational to Christianity in modern society. In evangelical Christianity, for instance, subjectivism is basic to the experience of salvation. Subjectivism is also basic in the existentialism of neo-orthodoxy.

Instrumental Religion. As religion loses its social importance but gains in individual significance, there emerges an emphasis on self-fulfillment, and not of self-denial for service, as a major function that religion should perform in modern society. Religion thus assumes an instrumental function, which the individual may or may not use in achieving personal fulfillment in a pluralistic, secular society. Religion may be utilized or dispensed with according to its instrumental value. In either event, society continues on, unaffected. The traditional values of self-denial and sacrifice are rarely stressed in the modern context, unless, of course, they somehow aid an individual to achieve personal integration and fulfillment.

Post-Industrial Religion. As modern, industrial society becomes post-industrial society, religion also becomes what we may term post-industrial religion. Several parallels can be drawn between post-industrial society and post-industrial religion. To begin with, post-industrial religion becomes, as society as a whole, "consumer-oriented". People attend religious services to be "fed", to be spiritually uplifted, and to leave with a feeling of emotional fulfillment. To maintain this expectation, services become more entertainment in nature than prophetic. To assure entertainment, and to meet the insatiable requirements of the religious consumer, experts assume a greater role in managing religion. Laymen meanwhile become more observers than participants. At this point, theoretical knowledge, and not traditional and prophetic teaching, becomes central in innovating change and formulating religious policy. Lastly, technology assumes a higher profile in the management and extension of religion, threatening to displace the more traditional forms of church structure and fellowship as avenues of religious expression. The so-called "electronic church" of U.S. society is the most prominent example of the emerging pre-eminence of technology in post-industrial religion.

Figure 7 above shows one final trend that religion in modern society may take, viz., cultism. Actually, cultism in modern society is more than a religious trend. Sociologically, a cult is a reaction both to the secularization of society and the counter-trend of making religion an individual and private matter. More specifically, a cult is a rejection of materialism and (secular) ideology, which function as substitute religions in modern society, and of the subjective consumer-oriented religion of individualism. These trends are rejected in favor of a more "group conscious" religion. A cult, to put it another way, represents a full circle return to the original functions of religion (defining the nature of transcendence, the destiny of the social group, and what should be the ultimate questions of life). By joining a cult an individual in modern society is in reality denying that government, education or any other social institution outside of religion has any right in fulfilling these essentially religious functions. These functions, in the view of the cultist, should be "reshifted" back to religion for their fulfillment in society; society is to regain its religious aura.

Cult and society therefore become one and the same, theologically. This development makes some severe sociological demands on individual members of a cult. They must, among other things, deny individual achievement and fulfillment in favor of building group cohesion and achieving group goals. As a group they must also separate themselves from modern society at large, because with its emphasis on secular pursuits and individual fulfillment, modern society is considered the arch-enemy. Without separation, modern society will erode both the religious values and the emphasis on group cohesion that the cult needs to survive; otherwise, individual members might drift back into modern society.

Not only does Figure 7 show the religious mosaic that is characteristic of modern society, it also displays the religious components of the cognitive map that individuals in modern society use to make sense of today's world. But since a number of these components are mutually exclusive, the actual cognitive map that exists for modern society is more complex than what Figure 7 indicates. For example, an individual as a member of modern society cannot both be secular in outlook and a member of a cult at the same time. Nor is it likely that an individual who has experienced a (subjective) religious conversion has also adopted a political ideology as a substitute religion. This does not mean that these mutually exclusive components do not exist together in the (modern) cognitive map of the world, for they do. Their co-existence, however, depends upon having different values, either a plus + or minus - in the cognitive map. If religion is [+ secular], then it is [-cult]; or if religion is [+ subjective], then it is also [-political ideology]. The converse is also possible, e.g., [- secular + cult] and [- subjective + political ideology]. When every component contained in Figure 7 is included, several configurations of pluses and minuses are possible.

The particular configuration of pluses and minuses that these components assume constitute the particular cognitive strategy that an individual in modern society uses for interpreting today's world. The cognitive strategy of a dedicated Marxist, for example, would contain the following configuration of values.

[+ secularization	- individualism]
[+ functional shift]	[- individualism]
[+ narrowing of role]	[- instrumental religion]
[+ substitute religion]	[- post-industrial religion]
	[- cult]

Figure 8

In this Marxist example the cognitive strategy for interpreting the world would be characterized as including the secularization of society and the elimination of individual religious expression. This strategy would also include the shifts of functions away from religion resulting in narrowing the role that religion plays in society. Marxist ideology would constitute a substitute religion, a condition that would exclude cultism from being a part of a Marxist's cognitive map.

There is one more dimension to the cognitive strategy that an individual uses to interpret today's world. That dimension is the individual's own interaction with that strategy. In Chapter 3 this individual interaction was termed cognitive style. One's interaction or style with a particular cognitive strategy for making sense of the world may range all the way from total conformity to rebellion. One's cognitive style, therefore, is more useful for purpose of communicating the Gospel, for it indicates the degree to which the person may be closed or open to the Gospel. Consider the Marxist and the cognitive strategy he is to use in interpreting the world. If he is in total agreement with that strategy then he would no doubt be closed to the Gospel. However, if he is in some degree deviant or in rebellion with the Marxist strategy, having meanwhile developed his own cognitive style for understanding the world, to that degree he may be open to the Gospel and the particular cognitive map of the world provided in the Scriptures.

"TAKE MY YOKE UPON YOU"

The previous two sections briefly described both the complexities of modern society and religion in modern society. Since religion is more crucial than other social institutions for communicating the Gospel cross-culturally in other societies, a question immediately comes to mind. Can the Gospel be adequately communicated in modern society? Since the Bible was written in another era under different social conditions, does the Bible contain any potential for modern society? In Chapter 6 and 7, we saw how the Bible could be communicated in tribal and peasant societies respectively. But those societies are much simpler in structure and culture and so contain many more correspondences to the social organization of Bible times. Modern society, however, is greatly more complex. Consequently, many have thought that the Gospel message can have no relevance for modern society unless it is "recontextualized" to correspond more with the way people in modern society make sense of the word.

Yet, we must remember, the Scriptures were not first proclaimed and written in uncomplicated times. The Scriptures serving as the heading of this section is an illustration in point. This Scripture, taken from Matthew 11, was first spoken in an urban context.

> Then he began to upbraid the cities where most of his mighty works had been done, because they did not repent. "Woe to you, Chorazin! woe to you Bethsaida! for if the mighty works done in you had been done in Tyre and Sidon, they would have repented long ago in sackcloth and ashes. But I tell you, it shall be more tolerable on the day of judgment for Tyre and Sidon than for you. And you, Capernaum, will you be exalted to heaven? You shall be brought down to Hades. For if the mighty works done in you had been done in Sodom, it would have remained until this day. But I tell you that it shall be more tolerable on the day of judgment for the land of Sodom than for you." (Mt. 11:20-24).

The three cities of Chorazin, Bethsaida and Capernaum formed a first century metropolitan strip along the northwest coast of the Sea of Galilee. It was a cosmopolitan area containing Jews and Gentiles, Roman garrison, troops and subjected people, tax-collectors and tax payers. Aramaic, Latin and Greek were common languages spoken in the streets, at the market places, and in homes. A major north-south highway ran through these cities connecting Jerusalem on the south and Caesarea Philippi on the north. Chorazin, Bethsaida and Capernaum, in addition, served as important trading centers for the Jewish population located to the west and for the Greek speaking population of the Decapolis area on the east.

It was in this metropolitan context that Jesus spent most of His time. In fact, Capernaum was called "his own city" (Mk. 2:1). So as we looked into the New Testament to discover how Jesus proclaimed the Gospel under peasant conditions, we may also look into this Scripture to discover how Jesus proclaimed the Gospel in an urban setting. Jesus' strategy for communicating the Gospel in this urban area is found in the verses immediately following the above quote.

> At that time Jesus declared, "I thank thee, Father, Lord of heaven and earth, that thou hast hidden these things from the wise and understanding and revealed them to babes; yea, Father, for such was thy gracious will. All things have been delivered to me by my Father; and no one knows the Son except the Father, and no one knows the Father except the Son and any one to whom the Son chooses to reveal him. Come to me, all who labor and are heavy laden, and I will give you rest. Take my yoke upon you, and learn from me; for I am gentle and lowly in heart, and you will find rest for your souls. For my yoke is easy, and my burden is light." (Mt. 11:25-30).

What makes these verses appropriate for demonstrating the potential of the Bible for proclamation in modern society is this: *they speak to the stresses of living in an urban, complex, pluralistic setting.*

There are stresses from living in tribal and peasant societies, but the burdens from modern living are in a real sense different in kind. Different kinds of adjustments are needed for modern society. Many, of course, make these adjustments but many others do not, or make less than perfect adjustments and so go through life suffering under various burdens. These burdens are both social and psychological in scope; they were present in the pluralistic setting of Capernaum and surrounding regions as they are present today in modern society. There are three burdens that individuals living in modern, pluralistic society must bear, and Jesus' invitation in Matthew 11:25-30 speaks to each of them.

Loneliness. Modern society is mass society, replete with mass communications, mass transit, mass education, mass advertisement, and even mass evangelism. But being one in a crowd can be a lonely experience. This can be true for both the individual born and reared in an urban setting and for the adult recently moved to the city from a rural background. Friends can offset loneliness, but friendship, in mass society is an impermanent thing; people shift from one person to another in forming friendships. The significance of Jesus' invitation is His offer of friendship—of sharing His burden in place of our own—in the task of living in modern society. It is the same offer Jesus made to His disciples: "No longer do I call you servants. . . . but I have called you friends" (Jn. 15:15). Jesus encased the message of the Gospel with an offer of friendship to those individuals caught in the loneliness of mass society.

Depersonalization. Loneliness in mass society can produce a crisis of identity. If an individual cannot relate to others in a close and personal way, then doubts about his identity emerge. And where a loss of identity occurs, feelings of depersonalization follow. But loss of identity and depersonalization also stems from other areas of modern living. Social role, for example, provides identity and feelings of being a person—of being somebody—in society, but if there are too many roles to negotiate or there are drastic changes in roles, both of which can happen in modern society, identity can become lost in an confused maze of conflicting roles, another condition that leads to feelings of loss of personhood. Another source of depersonalization is the need for *impersonal* transactions among individuals in modern society. In buying groceries at a supermarket, for example, the relationship between the shopper and store as represented by an employee, is contractual: the shopper agrees to pay for what he has selected and once the transaction is completed there is no more obligation between the two. While this may be a more efficient way to conduct business in mass society, it nevertheless contributes to depersonalization. The significance of Jesus' invitation, on the other hand, is an invitation to identify with Him. "I am gentle and lowly in heart" Jesus said. His invitation amounts to a restoration of personhood in a society that depersonalizes. It is perhaps no surprise, then, that in Antioch of Syria, the third largest city of the Roman Empire, the followers of Jesus Christ were first called Christians (Acts 11:26). They had identified themselves so much with Jesus Christ that even to outsiders they should henceforth be publicly identified as Christians.

Delegitimization. Perhaps the most difficult burden to bear in modern society is the delegitimization of behavior; no longer is right right or wrong wrong. What was once right now may or may not be right. And what was once wrong may now be considered the right thing to do. As a result, traditional authority, in the form of institutions and leaders, is undermined. Pluralism is at the root of delegitimization in modern society. On the one hand, because different customs and beliefs coexist in a single area, pluralism is a necessity if modern society is to be maintained. On the other hand, learning to live in a pluralistic society, while managing at the same time to maintain one's ethics and values, is a difficult task. It is a task, moreover, that many in modern society find impossible to fulfill. They compromise their values and in the end feel their life is no longer legitimate, or, in the words of the Apostle Paul, their conscience has become seared to the point where they no longer care (1 Tim. 4:2). The significance of Jesus' invitation is that it "relegitimizes" living morally in modern society. Jesus invited people to share His yoke and burden and find rest for their souls. Living righteously is a yoke, but it can be a harsh yoke if there is no legitimate reason for doing so. Becoming a follower of Jesus, however, legitimizes both the choice to live righteously and the behavior that flows from that choice.

The above Scripture from Matthew 11 suggests the basic strategy the cross-cultural communicator should follow in proclaiming the Gospel in modern society. The Gospel is addressed to individuals— "Come to me, all who labor and are heavy laden"—but not to individuals without taking into account the stresses of living in a complex, pluralistic social setting. Indeed, Jesus' invitation specifically addresses those problems while at the same time providing the solution—"take my yoke upon you, and learn from me."

But communicating the Gospel in modern society must not stop here; otherwise, the Gospel will end up as post-industrial religion. The Gospel is meant to do more than to turn individuals into religious consumers, where they show up at church to be fed and find personal wholeness. Personal wholeness is but one result of the Gospel. There is a greater wholeness that also must result from proclaiming the Gospel to individuals in modern society. The communication of the Gospel must provide also the wider, sociological framework wherein personal integration can take place. A broader communicative strategy—a strategy that must not stop at personal wholeness—is required. If the Gospel is to be successfully communicated in modern society, it must be "packaged" sociologically and not only individually.

James H. Jauncey stresses this need for packaging the Gospel sociologically for modern society.

> Initially it may appear that this is all there is to man: that his skin is the boundary of his being. But this is far from the truth. His personality reaches out to the environment in which he lives and most particularly, to the persons who inhabit that environment . . . Any evangelism, therefore, that treats man as a detached individual and does not consider him in relationship to others will be geared to a completely false situation. It will find it hard to reach him in the first place and, even if it does, will not be able to lay claim to his total life, such as conversion demands. (1972:23)

Jauncey goes on to give four ways by which the Gospel in modern society can indeed claim all of life.

Evangelism through social units. Since an individual does not exist autonomously but as a member of a social unit, it is with the social unit where evangelism must begin. The first social unit we must begin with, Jauncey states, is the family. As a matter of strategy in conversion, a person's family must be included: otherwise conversion will only enhance further the social fragmentation under which the individual is already suffering.

The need to belong to a group. A serious burden of modern living is being "groupless." Few individuals in modern society can manage to live autonomously. Most have a need to belong to a group. Evangelism, therefore, should show how this need can be fulfilled in Jesus Christ and His church. As a strategy, Jauncey writes that

> All this adds up to the fact that the person to be won for Christ is an individual-in-a-group or an individual-needing-a-group . . . evangelization can only be meaningful in that setting. (1972:27)

Cause hunger. Human beings must live for something that is outside of themselves. "We are born crusaders," Jauncey says. The emphasis on self in modern society, however, militates against this hunger for something greater than self. This creates still another burden under which individuals must live. The Gospel, though, can provide that something which people can live for. In evangelization, then, the Gospel must be commmunicated with the view of fulfilling cause hunger in the individual.

Identification through belonging to a Christian group. Without belonging to a group, a person suffers a loss of identity in modern society. From a sociological perspective it is not surprising to find in modern society a great number of voluntary associations, groups and organizations. In addition to being a born crusader, modern man is also a born joiner, because being a member of a group provides identity. Evangelistic strategy in modern society should therefore take advantage of this predisposition and present the church as the group through which an individual may gain an identity. As a further matter of strategy, Jauncey states that size is important in this regard: a large group, such as a large congregation, does not readily create the best conditions wherein an individual can gain an identity. A small group, such as a Sunday school class or a home Bible class, is more conducive for gaining an identity. In modern society, the Gospel should be communicated with the view of first directing individuals into small groups. "If it is a real live cohesive group," Jauncey states (p. 63), "conversion will be almost automatic."

To sum this chapter up: Just as in tribal and peasant societies, the potential of the Bible—hence the way the content of the Gospel is to be packaged sociologically—for modern society is found in the *koinonia* of the saints, the body of the believers who assemble together to form God's Kingdom on earth. It is the community of believers that provides the broader social context for communicating the Gospel in modern society. And it is through the community of believers that the stresses of living in modern society can truly be solved.

Chapter 9
Communicating The Gospel In Developing Societies

The elderly Thai grandmother listened politely as I explained why everyone, she included, must worship *phrachao* (the Thai word for God). When I had finished speaking, she grunted in agreement and proudly announced: "Every evening before I go to bed I do obeisance before the picture of the *phrachao* who lives down south."

Her response startled me, because it showed that her knowledge of Thai's social organization was from an earlier era of Thai history. Her interpretation of my message and the subsequent response were based on this outdated knowledge of how Thai society was organized: as I was explaining why she should worship *phrachao* (God) she was understanding my message in terms of paying respect to the King (also called *phrachao*) of Thailand whose residence was in Bangkok some 450 miles to the south of her village.

Formerly, the King of Thailand was considered divine by his subjects. This tradition, however, began to change when an English governess, Anna Leonowens, of *the King and I* fame, arrived in Bangkok in 1862 to tutor the royal children. Anna tutored the Crown Prince, Chulalongkorn, and as a result opened up for the Prince the world of western ideas. From this education, and with the encouragement of his father, King Mongkut, Chulalongkorn grew up determined to institute reforms that would bring Thailand into the modern era. Chulalongkorn became King of Thailand in 1868 and began immediately modernizing the governmental structures of Thailand. One far-reaching change Chulalongkorn implemented was the institution of a bureaucracy based not on royal kin but on merit and promotion through the civil service.

It was not until 1932, however, under the reign of King Prajadhipok, that the final change was made. In that year, Pridi Phanomyang, a brilliant Thai lawyer, led a bloodless coup that changed the government from an absolute to a constitutional monarchy. An Assembly, or parliament, was established out of which were appointed a prime minister and other high officials who were responsible for administrating the affairs of the nation.

This final social change has become a permanent feature of the way Thai society is organized. It is also an integral part of the cognitive map made available to Thai citizens for interpreting their world. For the most part this cognitive map is used by modern day Thai citizens, but there are isolated pockets in the outlying, rural areas of Thailand where the implications of this social change are not fully understood, especially by those born and reared before 1932 and who have had little if any formal education. The elderly grandmother above was one of these people (my conversation with her occurred in the early 1960's). For these people Thai society is still organized under a divine *phrachao* or king. Consequently, their communications and interpretations of messages are based on this perceived social organization.

This example from Thailand illustrates a common characteristic of developing nations, viz., social change is unevenly spread throughout society; its impact is not the same on all people. This chapter explores the nature of uneven social change plus the ramifications such holds for communicating the Gospel in today's world. This exploration is perhaps more timely than the chapters on tribal and modern societies; only the chapter on peasant society matches the importance of this chapter. This is because most developing countries also include peasant populations. So all the problems a missionary must take into account in communicating the Gospel in peasant societies are also present in developing nations. Indeed, these problems are often compounded because social development in a nation often creates in its wake new and additional dependent populations, e.g., those who benefit from social development (the elite) vs. those who are denied its fruits (peasants). Missionaries must consider these problems if the Gospel is to be adequately communicated in developing societies.

DEVELOPMENT: A CHARACTERIZATION

In Chapter 2 (The Sociological Imagination), development was briefly described in the context of social change and the tribal-modern continuum. Under social change, development was described in terms of the various functional shifts that occur among social institutions as a society changes, or "develops", from a more traditional, holistic, society to a modern, compartmentalized society. Such changes, especially as they affect religion and family, result in a society becoming modernized and secular. Social changes of this nature also produces cultural changes, i.e., changes in beliefs, norms, values and what is learned to be a member of society. Furthermore, as the relationships among social institutions change, so does the cognitive map for interpreting the world change. New cognitive strategies, as well as new cognitive styles, emerge in society.

Under the tribal-modern continuum, development was described as a continuum of change beginning with tribal society and moving through peasant society on to modern society. Figure 9 shows again the continuum of Chapter 2.

Tribal-Modern Continuum

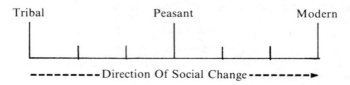

----------Direction Of Social Change---------►

Figure 9

In this view, development is a continuum of social change: there are degrees of change from a more holistic to a more compartmentalized society. Different societies, moreover, will be at different stages along the continuum, i.e., some societies are *undeveloped* (more tribal and traditional in culture) while others are developing (those someplace in the middle of the continuum). Still other societies are developed (those at the modern end of the continuum).

While development assumes that all of society changes, the emphasis is on changes that occur in the way a society is organized economically. Earlier, we stated that the social institution of economics performs three functions for the maintenance of society. First, economics establishes socially approved ways of exploiting, through investment and labor, various resources to produce goods and services. Second, economics provides ways of distributing goods and services. Lastly, economics define certain intangibles, such as what ceremonial activity should be associated with the production, exchange and consumption of goods. In undeveloped societies (some economists prefer to say underdeveloped), these functions are performed in traditional ways, while in developing and developed societies other methods considered more progresssive are pursued. One criterion employed to determined progress is the extent modern technology is utilized in fulfilling economic functions. Undeveloped societies, for example, rely on labor-saving technology that reduces the need for human labor in the production and distribution of goods and services. Developed societies rely mainly on technology with a minimum of human labor. Another criterion for determining progress is efficiency. Generally, the more labor-saving technology is used the more efficient the above economic functions can be performed. Figure 10 below illustrates how these two criteria are applied.

-------Degree of Technological Use for Fulfilling Functions------->

Functions	Undeveloped	Developing	Developed
Investment and Production	Human labor plus hand tools for exploiting the earth	Human labor augmented by animal and basis mechanical power for production	Heavy capital investment and extensive mechanization for production
Distribution	Human labor as a major means of transportation	Market and transportation system (animal and auto-motive)	Centralized market system; extensive transportation system (road, water, rail, air)
Ceremony	Sanctified by religious ritual	Informal, often kin based agreements	Formal and legally binding agreements

----------- Direction of Efficiency Rating for Fulfilling Functions ----------->

Figure 10

153

Technological development, especially in production and distribution, brings a society into the modern era. But society is not the only thing made modern by technological change. Individual members also undergo change, and, as a function of development, are similarly made modern. Alex Inkeles (1969:208), in researching the effects of change in several developing countries, states that there is a set of personal qualities, forming in his words a "syndrome of modernity", that emerges in people as they adjust to technological development in society.

> Central to this syndrome are (1) openness to new experience, both with people and with new ways of doing things such as attempting to control births; (2) the assertion of increasing independence from the authority of traditional figures like parents and priests and a shift of allegiance to leaders of government, public affairs, trade unions, cooperatives, and the like; (3) belief in the efficacy of science and medicine, and a general abandonment of passivity and fatalism in the race of life's difficulties; and (4) ambition for oneself and one's children to achieve high occupational and educational goals. Men who manifest these characteristics (5) like people to be on time and show an interest in carefully planning their affairs in advance. It is also part of this syndrome to (6) show strong interest and take an active part in civic and community affairs and local politics; and (7) to strive energetically to keep up with the news, and within this effort to prefer news of national and international import over items dealing with sports, religion, or purely local affairs.

Referring to Alex Inkeles' research on the effects of change in making individuals modern, Phillip E. Hammon et al (1975:79) add that

> In our day, a modern mentality in a "developing" society is enhanced by formal educational experiences and/or experiences in large-scale factory work. . . . In other times, not these but other experiences produced in people a tendency to welcome— or at least recognize and acknowledge—change in their societies. In every case this modern mentality involves disenchantment with (alienation from or a weakened commitment to) the past and present and a receptivity to new ways to achieve new goals; that is to say, the modern mentality, relative to its time and place, *rationalizes.*

This emphasis on economic development often produces an unevenness in the overall modernization of society: while the economic section of society is modernized and made more efficient, other sectors fall behind. There then develops in society what the sociologist William Fielding Ogburn (1922) termed culture lag. As family, religion and other social institutions fall behind, the culture values represented by these social institutions also lag behind. In industrialization, for example, the large family is no longer necessary, since children are not needed to work in the factory as they were on the farm. Yet cultural values may still dictate that a married couple produce and raise a number of children, all of whom must now be clothed, fed and educated over several years before they become productive members of society. The lag, moreover, may still persist even though birth control methods are available: the same cultural value dictating the large family may also function to prevent the use of birth control methods to limit family size.

There is one more consequence from the emphasis on economic development in society. Other social institutions tend to assume an instrumental role in the task of economic development. Instead of making contributions to the maintenance of society equal in importance to economics, the other social institutions function to advance the cause of economic development. The first social institution that often assumes this instrumental function in developing societies is government. Ironically though, in assuming an instrumental role, government does not decrease, as other social institutions do, in power and importance in maintaining society. On the contrary, government increases in power, becoming highly institutionalized and centralized with a large corps of specialists. Yet this power is still directed to advancing first the economic development of society.

At this stage a further consequence may occur as a result of the emphasis on economic development. Since economic development is the most important, if not pressing, goal to achieve, those in power may turn government into a totalitarian government as a short-cut to economic development. In becoming totalitarian, resources and labor can more readily be mobilized and manipulated to more quickly achieve economic goals. At this point the other social institutions (education, family, religion) become not only instrumental in serving economic ends in society but also become instrumental in serving and legitimizing the authoritarianism of government, especially in its goal of achieving economic progress. The family, for instance, is viewed not as the transmitter of traditional values to the oncoming generation but as the means of producing more labor for industry; indeed, the socialization role of the family may be viewed more as a detriment than a benefit to progress and so must be curtailed in favor of early and extended education outside the family in a formal school system.

To achieve economic progress in a society requires more than development in industrialization, production and transportation. Members of society must also be brought into this modern world, otherwise development in the economic sector will progress only so far. Modern technology and transportation systems require modern minds to operate. In order to gain modern minds as quickly as possible, the government of a developing society may adopt a modern political ideology from the west. Socialism and Marxism have been two such popular ideologies. In adopting a western ideology, it is hoped that it will quickly replace traditional belief and value systems, thus opening up the way for members of society, especially those who will constitute the workers and managers in industry, to become modern in outlook. At this point education assumes an instrumental function in promoting the new ideology as the quickest and surest path to economic development. Schools and universities must now teach the new ideology as the framework through which society and individuals will achieve modernization. Religion is also pressed into service at this point. Religious organizations and specialists are expected to support the new ideology, suppressing those religious doctrines that contradict the ideology and reinterpreting others to give further legitimacy to its adoption by government and subsequent transmission by education to a new generation.

The preceding briefly characterizes the classical view of development that has been in vogue since World War II when it was initiated by the industrialized nations of the West. When development was first implemented, there was hope that the then undeveloped nations would indeed become developed and enjoy the fruits of industrialization. Of course, there was often an underlying more self-protective, reason for this hope than pure altruism on the part of the western world. Economic development, many thought, was the best defense against communist influence and a nation's ultimately entering Russia's or China's sphere of control. The more nations kept out of the communist orbit, the safer the western world would be from wars and rebellions instigated by the communist powers in the name of Marxist-Leninist ideology.

This hope of development, with the possibility of one or two exceptions, unfortunately, has not been realized in nonwestern nations. There are many reasons for this failure, reasons too complicated to describe in the brief space of this section. Nevertheless, one reason stands out, viz., the failure of the past forty years stems from the fact that development was too narrowly conceived even in economic terms. The focus in development all too often was on technological innovations that would more quickly and efficiently meet essential human and societal needs. Little thought was given to other aspects of life and how technological innovations might also affect them. In other words, development was perceived in terms of new technology but without an accompanying ideology that would in turn relate the new technology to other aspects of life, showing in effect how and where technology fits in with other social institutions for the maintenace of society. For those undeveloped or developing societies having an ideology (or religion) that readily allowed innovations from the outside, new technology *sans* ideology posed few problems of adjustments. But for those societies that had ideologies or religions restricting outside innovations, technology, without an accompanying framework to show its relation to all of life, often proved disruptive.

Technology, of course, is neutral with respect to ideology and religion. Yet it is this neutrality, ironically enough, that all too often accounts for the persistent popularity of Marxism (and even Marxism-Leninism, or communism, in some instances) in many developing nations, because it is Marxism, despite its economic and political disasters in other nations, that provides an interpretive framework for relating new and foreign technology to all of life, including how it fits in historically and eschatologically in the social evolution of man. Technology (e.g., industrialization, modernization, etc.) in Marxism, to state it another way, is not autonomous and unrelated to other areas of life but is an integral part of man's pilgrimage toward the millenium. Because it is primarily an interpretive framework, Marxists find it easy to excuse the failures of Marxism to achieve true economic development and political freedom in today's world. Such failures are due to imperfect or incomplete application of the framework and not to the imperfections inherent in the framework. This, too, adds to the continual popularity of Marxism in today's world of developing nations.

The emphasis on ideology as a comprehensive interpretive framework signals a subtle change in the use of ideology in developing nations. This is especially true for Marxism. Above we noted that in an earlier time ideology was conceived as an instrument for modernization, both for society and as a framework whereby people could more readily think in modern terms in order to make full use of modern technology. By creating more modern individuals, it was thought, society would develop faster. But with the failure of development, ideology had to assume a new role. Instead of being a neutral instrument for achieving modernization, ideology has become a charter for social revolution in the developing world. That is, since developing nations do not correspond to the interpretive framework, as outlined by ideology, development will be impossible; there is need first for radical social change so there will be such correspondence. Only then, it is argued, will development as originally conceived be successful. Marxism and liberation theology are two ideologies currently being promoted as charters for social revolution, another factor that adds to their persistent popularity in today's world.

This discussion on the changing role of ideology in the developing world brings us full circle back to peasant society. The reason for this is not difficult to see. It is the peasant societies of the world that have received much of the economic aid for development from the industrialized nations of the West. But after several decades of western aid, peasant societies appear no better off economically than before. It is not surprising, then, that it is in peasant societies where Marxism and liberation theology have received the most attention and where they are now being promoted as charters for social revolution. The ramifications of this fact of communicating the gospel cross-culturally in today's world are the same as those discussed in the chapter on peasant society.

RELIGION IN DEVELOPING SOCIETY

In the preceding section we noted that development focuses on economics and government followed by education. In Chapter II we made the observation that even though a society develops along the lines of economics, government and education, it does not follow that the social institutions of family and religion automatically develop (i.e., become modernized) to the same extent or in the same manner. Indeed, such is usually not the case, especially for religion. Religion in developing society often lags behind development in other social institutions. Individual members of developing society may be capable of discussing economics and government in modern terms, but may still be tribal or peasant in thinking when it comes to religion. Consequently, a model different from the one used in preceding chapters is required for characterizing religion in developing society.

In those chapters religion was described in terms of [+ holistic + compartmentalized + important]. In developing society, however, the relationship between religion and the rest of society is much more of a mixed bag. Religion is no longer just 'plus-or-minus' holistic, etc.; it falls someplace in between. Religion has no clear-cut relationship, or interdependency, with other social institution in the maintenance of society. Religion may yet function in maintaining the traditional aspects of society, but as economics, government and education develop to include the complex aspects of modern life, the relationship between religion on the one hand and economics, government and education on the other, becomes blurred and confused.

The model needed is one that will display the development of religion in relation to the development of other social institutions. Figure 11 is such a model displayed in graph form. The graph is meant to characterize a hypothetical society only and not some actual society. Figure 11 shows to what degree each social institution has developed away from the holistic nature found in tribal society to the institutionalized and compartmentalized nature found in modern society. Government, for example, is at [.6] along the scale of development while economics is at nearly [.8]. Education is equal with government at [.6] but family is not quite to [.5] while religion is the least developed of all at [.4]. That is to say, religion is the least institutionalized and compartmentalized of all social institutions. There are, as the graph shows, areas of social life still containing a religious dimension: these areas are the traditional aspects of society. But as the graph also shows, there are other areas (represented by the portions of the bars extending on beyond the bar proceeding from religion) that have no religious dimensions. These are areas that have developed beyond what religion in its traditional form can include.

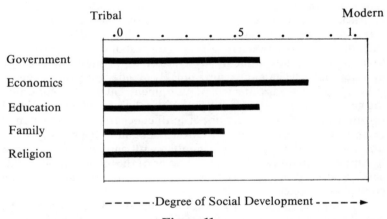

Figure 11

From a functional viewpoint Figure 11 shows the functional load each social institution carries in the total maintenance of our hypothetical developing society. As society develops, not only do functions shift away from religion to other social institutions, but new and additional functions (the product of technological and ideological innovations from the outside) come to be associated with those institutions developing the most. This has the effect of "loading" these institutions (government and economics) with still more functions, some very crucial for maintaining a constant rate of development. Such additional loading produces still another effect in the overall organization of society, viz., the functional role of religion in maintaining society decreases, in net terms, even further than what normally occurs in just functional shifts alone.

There are several consequences that may follow from these effects. First, as other social institutions develop, religion often becomes ill-equipped in providing a plausible framework whereby members of society can assimilate modern technology and ideas into their lives. When this happens, members of society, especially those who have become modern, consider their society's religion as outdated, stifling, too conservative, etc. At this point a culture lag between religion and the rest of society is felt, and as society develops even further in government and economics, an even wider gap emerges between society and religion. This gap is similar in nature to the void created in modern society by certain religious functions becoming associated with other social institutions. In either case the void, or gap, must be filled by something that can take the place of religion.

Many times this gap in developing society is filled by secularization (as in modern society). At other times it may be filled by a political or economic ideology that explicitly provides the broader framework for assimilating modern technology and ideas. If the culture lag or gap between religion and the rest of society is perceived to be great, then government may aggressively promote an ideology in order to fill the gap, thus more quickly ameliorating the effects of culture lag in the task of social development. Such intervention by the government sometimes conflicts with religion and its traditional role in society. If a great amount of conflict occurs, government may respond in one of two ways. Government may back away from promoting an ideology that is in conflict with religion, or it may seek to suppress religion even further in favor of the ideology. The latter case, if pursued, results in government becoming totalitarian in its control over society.

The graph of Figure 11 also shows the important categories of the cognitive map available to individual members of developing society for making sense of the world. These categories, however, are not the various social institutions, as one might conclude from the graph. Rather, the categories are the relationships—more precisely the degree of interdependency—holding between the various social institutions in the overall task of maintaining society. Instead of having a plus-or-minus value, a number (showing the degree of functional interdependency) is assigned to each social institution. Figure 12 illustrates the cognitive map that is available for members of our hypothetical society of Figure 11.

[.6 Government]   [.5 Education]

[.8 Economics]   [.4 Family]

[.3 Religion]

Figure 12

That is, the heavier functional load for interpreting the world is placed on government and economics, and how far these two social institutions have progressed. The other three social institutions have lighter functional loads in interpreting the world. Religion, at [.3], has the lightest functional load in this interpretative task.

Obviously, as a cognitive map made available to members of our hypothetical society, the social institutions of Figure 12 are subject to changing numerical values as more development occurs. Economics at [.8], for example, may increase to [.9], in which case government may increase to [.7], or better. And at the other end of the scale religion may decrease to [.2], i.e., religion is used even less in interpreting the meaning of the world. (On the other hand, religion may increase in *individual* value as in modern society.) The reverse may also occur. A government hostile to development may arise in a developing society and succeed in slowing, if not reversing, the progress to modernity. In this case economics may fall back to [.5] and in response religion may increase to [.4], i.e., economics is used less and religion more in making sense of the world.

Because of the changing nature of developing society, the cognitive strategies that various individual groups use for interpreting the world are also subject to constant change. The cognitive strategy for males, as an example, who are normally more exposed to the effects of progress and modernization, will differ from the cognitive strategy for females who are least exposed. Assuming Figure 12 to be representative of the cognitive strategy for males, let us assume that Figure 13 represents the cognitive strategy for females in a developing society.

[.5 Government]   [.4 Education]

[.5 Economics]   [.7 Family]

[.7 Religion]

Figure 13

For females, family and religion figure more in making sense of the world while government, economics and education figure least.

The cognitive strategy for the elite and progressive in society will in similar fashion differ from the one used by the uneducated masses. Again, assuming that Figure 12 is representative of the cognitive strategy for the elite and educated of our developing society, Figure 14 would represent the cognitive strategy for the masses.

[.6 Government]   [.4 Education]

[.5 Economics]   [.7 Family]

[.6 Religion]

Figure 14

For the uneducated masses, government would outrank economics in interpreting the world, and family and religion would outrank all social institutions in the same task.

But regardless of the individual or group involved, cognitive strategies must in the end be open-ended systems. Developing society is subject to change too much for it to be otherwise. People, regardless of status or role, must be capable of taking into account new developments and changes and on such a basis form new cognitive strategies for making sense (once again!) of the world.

Individuals in developing society react to the changes that constantly occur in their lives. Such reaction results in each individual forming his own cognitive style in response to change and progress. An individual, for instance, may react favorably to the economic development that is occurring and thus may be open to even more change or faster development than what is taking place. At the other end an individual may react unfavorably to the development and modernization that is happening and thus may try to obstruct or even prevent such changes. Other individuals may react favorably to some changes that are taking place while simultaneously reacting unfavorably to other changes. It is the individual's cognitive style, developed in response to progress and modernization, that holds the more promising ramifications for communicating the Gospel in developing societies.

"LEAVE THE DEAD TO BURY THE DEAD"

What is the potential of the Bible for proclamation in developing societies? Does the Bible have anything to "say" within the conditions found in developing nations? From one perspective the answer is yes: insofar as a developing society corresponds to the conditions found in tribal, peasant and modern societies—societies where we have already see that the Gospel is indeed relevant—then the Bible has something to say. But there is a special, more dynamic dimension to developing society. There is change and movement away from one social type to another. This dynamic aspect establishes a different type of question regarding the relevancy of the Bible than what is present in tribal, peasant and modern societies, viz., what is the potential of the Bible for proclamation in changing times? Does the Gospel remain relevant as societies and individuals move away from more traditional ways of living to the complexities of modern life?

These questions are pertinent in a special sense because of the way religion is often viewed in today's world of change and development. Religion is viewed more often than not as a conservative force in society, holding back, if not obstructing, progress toward modernity. Inasmuch as religion functions in this manner, it is an opponent to change. Such a function is not all bad, however, for some social change may indeed not be good for society. Without such a conservative force, society could be in trouble. But unfortunately, religion often turns out to be an obstruction to certain changes that are necessary and inevitable in this age of modern technology and new methods for accomplishing individual and social needs. This obstruction can create, or make greater, the culture lag between religion and the rest of society as discussed above. If such obstruction persists, the conclusion may be drawn that religion has no relevancy, i.e., has nothing to say in an age of development and technological innovation.

The same conclusion is often drawn with regards to the Bible. While the Scriptures may speak to those areas of life in developing society that are yet traditional, they have nothing to say to those areas that have developed beyond the traditional. If this conclusion is accepted, then there is nothing to be communicated from the Bible that in reality can speak to a society in the midst of social change and development. This conclusion is wrong. The biblical message, the Good News of Jesus Christ, does contain potential for proclamation in developing nations. One such potential is found in the text from which the heading to this section is taken, Luke 9:57-62.

> As they were going along the road, a man said to him, "I will follow you wherever you go." And Jesus said to him "Foxes have holes, and birds of the air have nests; but the Son of man has nowhere to lay his head." To another he said, "Follow me." But he said, "Lord, let me first go and bury my father." But he said to him, "Leave the dead to bury their own dead; but as for you, go and proclaim the kingdom of God." Another said, "I

will follow you, Lord; but let me first say farewell to those at my home." Jesus said to him, "No one who puts his hand to the plow and looks back is fit for the kingdom of God."

The potential for communicating the Gospel in developing society is found in three points that Jesus Christ makes in this text.

The uncertainty of the future. A developing society is constantly changing under the impact of new technological and ideological innovations. Such continual change can be exhilarating, but it also has a troubling dimension: the future is no longer predictable as in tribal or peasant society. Now the significance of the above text in this regards is that Jesus did not promise future predictability to those who follow Him. The foxes may have holes, and the birds may have nests, but He had no place to lay His head. Following Jesus requires change, and as with any change (except in an eternal sense) it leads into a future that can be perceived only dimly. Yet, while the future may not be fully knowable, Jesus invites individuals to follow Him as the future unfolds.

Leave the present to enter the future. In social development the present must never become sufficient unto itself; there is always more progress to be made. This need to leave the present to enter the future performs two essential functions in the modernization of individuals: it serves to break down traditional orientations and in their place establish an orientation toward the future. The person whom Jesus called in the above text asked leave to first bury his father—a request that could have taken some time to accomplish, depending on whether his father was still living or not. Jesus' response, however, was not sympathetic to the present reality of the man's situation: "Leave the dead to bury their own dead." Rather, Jesus commanded him to enter the future: "but as for you, go and proclaim the kingdom of God." It was a command to leave the security of the present (of staying at home) to enter an insecure future (by leaving home before his father's death he might forfeit any right to his part of the inheritance). Yet, as in the first point above, Jesus' command implies an invitation to trust Him for security as the future unfolds.

No turning back. Once a society is charted on the road to progress, there is no turning back. Of course, there may be temporary setbacks—for example, religious fanatics may force a resurgence of traditional values—but the benefits of modern technology are too great to be delayed for long. This is especially true with respect to modern medicines and medical technology. Regardless of religious beliefs, better health and prolonged life, two things made possible by modern technology, are desired by individuals. Yet, as more people live longer because of improved health, new pressures for more modern technology are created. A larger population, for example, must now be fed and, more crucially, employed in nonfarm jobs. These two needs can be met by turning back the clock of progress and immediately reducing population, or by proceeding forward into modern agricultural technology to produce more food and into industrialization to create more jobs. The former is morally and politically impossible to do, even though Marxist-Leninist societies, often in a de facto fashion, manage to reduce their population through executions, slave-labor camps (where many people die) and a highly regimented life that in the end tends to reduce the birth rate. The only option left for a developing society is for continual development and modernization. This was the option Jesus gave to a would-be disciple who asked permission to turn back in order to bid farewell to his kin. To turn back, after putting his hand to the plow, would make the disciple unfit for the Kingdom.

It is of interest here to note that Luke is the only Gospel writer to have grouped these three points together into one text. Matthew 8:18-22 has only the first two points. The significance of this observation perhaps lies more in what it shows about Luke than in the "orderly account" (Lk. 1:3) of the three conversations contained in this text. These conversations show that Luke himself was future oriented, an observation that corresponds to what we can deduce from Luke's background. Being an educated Gentile, Luke no doubt was forward-looking and not tradition bound. Similarly, in being a convert to a religion whose origin was among the Jews of Palestine, he no doubt considered his conversion as a forward step in his life.

The three points taken from Luke 9:57-62 suggest what should be included in a strategy for communicating the Gospel cross-culturally in developing societies. There are three parts to this strategy.

Religious Social Psychology. Social psychology is the study of the interaction between the individual and his social environment: the role that social environment plays in shaping personality structure (attitudes, belief, etc.) and how the individual adapts to his social environment. As a discipline, social psychology describes all of society's effects upon the individual. For our purposes here, however, we need to focus only on the role religion as a social institution plays in shaping personality and what adaptations are made on the part of the individual to this role. This is especially crucial in developing societies where the social institutions of government and economics exert an ever increasing influence on individuals while religion tends to exert less influence in shaping people's lives. Yet, as was seen in the graph of Figure 11, there are areas of life in developing society that are still considered traditional and in which religion still functions in important ways to maintain society. But whether an individual has "accepted" the validity of the traditional in his life is another matter; he may have, in which case he is more traditional in outlook, or he may not have, in which case he is more modern in outlook. All this adds up to an important first question that a missionary must answer before he proclaims the Gospel to an individual in a developing society: *Is the individual tribal, peasant or modern in his religious attitudes and behavior?* If the individual is more tribal or holistic in outlook, then a communicative strategy showing the holistic nature of the gospel is needed. But if the individual has moved from a holistic outlook to a compartmentalized outlook, but in which religion is still important, then a comparable strategy is needed to show how the Gospel is similarly important in life. And if the individual is modern in outlook, having rejected the traditional part of society, then a communicative strategy showing the relevancy of the Gospel for solving the stresses of modern living is needed.

An emphasis on change. Regardless of where an individual is in terms of tribal, peasant or modern orientations to life, change is still a fact of life in a developing society. Whatever one's orientation is at any one time, it will undoubtedly be different in the future. New technologies and innovations will assure it. Consequently, in communicating the Gospel in a developing society, social change should be an important part of the "sociological package" in which the message of the Gospel is wrapped for proclamation. Just as communicative strategy in previous chapters took into account the "static" aspects of tribal, peasant and modern society respectively, so must communicative strategy for developing society take into account the dynamics of social change in developing society. The Gospel, on entering society from the outside, is an innovation, and as such the cross-cultural communicator of the Gospel should tap the dynamics of development for its proclamation. Since individuals in developing societies are undergoing change anyway, the progress of their change should be under the direction of the Good News of Jesus Christ.

"In him all things have their proper place" (Col 1:17 TEV). The path along which change should be directed leads toward Jesus Christ. But the path does not lead to belief in and acceptance of Jesus Christ as personal savior alone. The change must also lead to Jesus Christ as the hermeneutic for all of life and by which all things new and old find their rightful place. In other words, the Gospel message, in order to be packaged in a sociologically relevant manner, must provide the social framework through which new technologies and innovations may be integrated into life. For if the Gospel cannot accomplish this, then it may be rejected by many in developing society as being no better equipped for the modern world than their traditional religion. Listeners of the Gospel message, who are

members of developing society, must be able to see how social change finds its proper place in Jesus Christ.

While social change must form the sociological side to content in communicating the Gospel message in developing society, social change must not be directionless or random. The social change that is encoded along with content must direct listeners to the social relationships to be found with God and with one another in the church. The church, as the Kingdom of God on earth, is the proper goal of social change in the communication of the Gospel to individuals in developing nations. In a developing nation individuals as well as society are changing. The Gospel message, as proclaimed in changing society, must therefore encompass change and transformation, both in the person and in the relationships that the person has with others. Such change and renewal are found first and last in the church.

Chapter 10
Tying It Together

Throughout Part II we have emphasized the church as the proper sociological package in which the content of the Gospel is wrapped for communication cross-culturally in other societies. This emphasis stems from the way message was defined in Chapter I. There we noted that a message is composed of two parts: content plus details of social organization. Both are necessary in communicating a message; a communicator cannot escape or delete the sociological aspect of communicating a message, nor does the receiver of a message filter out the sociological aspect on receiving a message in order to receive only content. Not only are both content and sociological packaging necessary in the construction and interpretation of a message, but both are also necessary in transmitting meaning during communication. From content one type of meaning is communicated, and from the sociological details another type of meaning is communicated. Both are interwoven, more precisely encoded, to form a message for transmission, and at the receiving end both are unraveled or decoded. As content and details of social organization are encoded together to form a single message, moreover, rules of appropriateness are observed: the sociological package must be appropriate to the content to be communicated, and vice versa. At the receiving end, on decoding a message into its constituent parts, an interpretation of the appropriateness of the sociological package to content is also made. If an inappropriate relationship is perceived, i.e., the rules of appropriateness are not observed in encoding and transmitting the message, then the message may be misunderstood or rejected.

Since details of social organization are unavoidable in communicating messages, including the Gospel message, an important question is raised for the cross-cultural communicator of the Gospel. What is the appropriate sociological package for the content of the Gospel for proclamation in another society? The answer to this question, as we have pointed out during the course of this book, depends upon the *type* of society where the Gospel is to be proclaimed. Since there are different types of societies, we have argued, there is a different appropriate sociological package for each type.

This is because, as we have observed throughout Part II, details of social organization differ from one social type to another. Within such differences, however, we have maintained that the content side of the Gospel message remains constant: otherwise the Gospel would be in no position to "speak" to the cultural condition of each social type we have discussed.

At this point in the process, we also claimed, communication of the Gospel reduces to strategy of communication; more precisely communication reduces to formulating and implementing a strategy for encoding and transmitting along with content, the particular sociological package appropriate for the type of society where the Gospel message is to be proclaimed. By such a strategy being implemented, the Gospel stands a better change of being understood in another social context, because members of this other social context are, as they decode the Gospel message, interpreting the appropriateness of content and sociological packaging woven together by the missionary communicator. And when the Gospel is thus judged appropriate, the missionary communicator stands a better chance of persuading individuals to accept Jesus Christ as Lord.

For each social type in Part II we discussed examples of the appropriateness between sociological package and content, of strategy in achieving such appropriateness in communication, and examples of the potential in the Bible for communicating such

Meaning of the Church for communicating the
Gospel according to Social Type

"The Church is the appropriate social unit . . .

Tribal Society	that provides community support for tribal believers."
Peasant Society	where social justice is at last found for peasant believers."
Modern Society	where stresses of modern life are lightened for believers."
Developing Society	where change and renewal in social relationships are ultimately realized for believers."

Figure 15

appropriateness in the society under discussion. In each instance we ended up by stating that the church, as the Kingdom of God on earth, is the proper sociological package for commmunicating the Gospel. That is, those details of social organization that are necessary in communication find their ultimate realization in the fellowship of those who believe. But in stating this we must notice one thing. As details of social organization differ from one social type to another so does the realization differ. In other words, the church, as a fellowship of believers and where appropriate details of social organization are realized in communication, assumes a different cultural meaning from one social type to another. Figure 15 summarizes these differences in meaning for the church as the Gospel is communicated in different societies.

Figure 15 summarizes all of Part II and its emphasis on formulating culturally sensitive strategies for communicating the Gospel in today's world. But while it summarizes Part II, we must remember that it is only a summary, illustrating what needs to be done in cultural interpretation and planning communicative strategies for proclaiming the Gospel in different social contexts. Much more than what was presented in these few chapters need to be done if the Gospel is to be adequately proclaimed in today's world. Yet, to the extent that principles of culture interpretation and strategies of communication have been illustrated, to that extent Part II is successful.

References

Arndt, William F. and F. Wilber Gingrich 1957. *A Greek-English Lexicon of the New Testament and other Early Christian Literature*. Chicago: University of Chicago Press.

Arnold, Dean E. 1975. The New Ethnography. In *Encyclopedia of Anthropology*. David E. Hunter and Phillip Whitten, eds., New York: Harper & Row.

Bell, Daniel 1973. *The Coming of the Post-Industrial Society*. New York: Basic Books.

Beyerhaus, Peter 1971. *Missions—Which Way?* Grand Rapids, MI: Zondervan.

Blumer, Herbert 1969. *Symbolic Interactionism*. Englewood Cliff, NJ: Prentice-Hall, Inc.

Cuzzort, R.P. and E.W. King 1976. *Humanity and Modern Social Thought, Second Edition*. Hinsdale, IL: The Dryden Press.

Dressler, David with Donald Carns 1969. *Sociology, The Study of Human Interaction*. New York: Alfred A. Knopf.

Easton, David 1959. Political Anthropology. In *Biennial Review of Anthropology* by Bernard J. Siegal, Stanford, CA: Stanford University Press.

Evans-Pritchard, E.E. 1965. *Theories of Primitive Religion*. London: Oxford University Press.

Federica, Ronald C. 1970. *Sociology*. Reading, MA: Addison-Wesley.

Filbeck, David 1964. Concepts of Sin and Atonement Among the Thai. *Practical Anthropology* 11:181-184.

_____ 1973. Pronouns In Northern Thai. *Anthropological Linguistics* 15:345-361.

Firth, Raymond 1971. *Elements of Social Organization 3rd Ed.* London: Tavistock.

_____ 1973. *Symbols, Public and Private*. Ithaca, NY: Cornell University Press.

Fishman, Joshua A. 1972. *Sociolinguistics, A Brief Introduction*. Rowley, MA: Newbury House Publishers.

Fodor, Jerry A. 1975. *The Language of Thought*. Cambridge, MA: Harvard University Press.

Fortes, M. and E.E. Evans-Pritchard 1940. *African Political Systems.* London: Oxford University Press.

Foster, George M. 1967. Introduction: What Is a Peasant? In *Peasant Society, A Reader.* Jack M. Fotter, May N. Diaz, George M. Foster, Eds., Boston: Little, Brown and Co.

Friedl, John 1976. *Cultural Anthropology.* New York: Harper's College Press.

Garbarino, Merwyn S. 1977. *Sociocultural Theory in Anthropology.* New York: Harper & Row.

Geertz, Clifford 1973. *The Interpretation of Cultures.* New York: Basic Books.

Goffman, Ervin 1971. *Strategic Interaction.* Philadelphia: University of Pennsylvania Press.

Gutierrez, Gustave 1973. *A Theology of Liberation.* Maryknoll, NY: Orbis Books.

Hammon, Phillip E., Louis Wolf Goodman, Scott Creer, Richard H. Hall, and Mary Catherine Taylor 1975. *The Structure of Human Society.* Lexington, MA: D.C. Heath and Co.

Hansen, Judith Friedman 1979. *Sociocultural Perspectives on Human Learning: An Introduction to Educational Anthropology.* Englewood Cliffs, NJ: Prentice Hall, Inc.

Inkeles, Alex 1969. Making Men Modern: On the Causes and Consequences of Individual Changes in Developing Countries. *American Journal of Sociology* 75:308-211.

_____ and David Smith 1974. *Becoming Modern: Individual Changes in Six Developing Countries.* Cambridge, MA: Harvard University Press.

Jauncey, James H. 1972. *Psychology for Successful Evangelism.* Chicago: Moody Press.

Katz, Daniel 1960. The Functional Approach to the Study of Attitudes. *Public Opinion Quarterly* 24:163-204.

Kennedy, John G. 1977. *Struggle for Change in a Nubian Community.* Palo Alto, CA: Mayfield Publishing Co.

Kroeber, A.L. 1948. *Anthropology.* New York: Harcourt Brace Javanovich.

Light, Donald, Jr. and Suzanne Keller 1975. *Sociology.* New York: Alfred A. Knopf.

Luzbetak, Louis J. 1970. *The Church and Cultures.* Techny, IL: Divine Word Publications.

Malinowski, Bronislaw 1920. Kula: The Circulating Exchange of Valuables in the Archipelagoes of Eastern New Guinea. *Man* 51:97-105.

McGavran, Donald 1970. *Understanding Church Growth.* Grand Rapids, MI: William B. Eerdmans Publishing Co.

Mercer, Elaine E. and Jules J. Wanderer 1970. *The Study of Sociology.* Belmont, CA: Wadsworth Publishing Co.

Merton, Robert K. 1964. Bureaucratic Structure and Personality. In *Personality and Social Systems.* Neil J. Smelser and William T. Smelser, eds. New York: John Wiley and Sons, Inc.

Miquez-Bonino, Jose 1975. *Doing Theology in a Revolutionary Situation.* Philadelphia: Fortress Press.

Mills, C. Wright 1959. *The Sociological Imagination.* London: Oxford University Press.

Murphy, Robert E. 1979. *An Overture to Social Anthropology.* Englewood Cliffs, NJ: Prentice-Hall, Inc.

Nida, Eugene 1960. *Message and Mission.* South Pasadena, CA: William Carey Library.

Ogburn, William Fielding 1922. *Social Changes: With Respect to Culture and Original Nature.* New York: Huebsch.

Padilla, Rene 1975. Evangelism and the World. In *Let The Earth Hear His Voice,* J.D. Douglas, Ed. Minneapolis, MN: World Wide Publications.

Pi-Sunyar, Oriol and Zdenek Salzmann 1978. *Humanity and Culture: An Introduction to Anthropology.* Boston: Houghton Mifflin Co.

Redfield, Robert 1941. *Folk Culture of Yucatan.* Chicago: University of Chicago Press.

_____ 1953. *The Primitive World and Its Transformation.* Ithaca, NY: Cornell University Press.

_____ 1955. The Social Organization of Tradition. The Far East Quarterly XV No. 15.

_____ 1956. *Peasant Society and Culture.* Chicago: University of Chicago Press.

_____ 1960. *The Little Community and Peasant Society and Culture.* Chicago: University of Chicago Press.

Schwarz, Henry A. 1976. Social Anthropology. In *Encyclopedia of Anthropology.* David E. Hunter and Phillip Whitten, eds. New York: Harper & Row.

Scott, Waldron 1975. The Task Before Us. *Let The Earth Hear His Voice.* J.D. Douglas, ed. Minneapolis, MN: World Wide Publications.

Schaeffer, Frances 1976. *The God Who Is There.* Downers Grove, IL: InterVarsity Press.

Strykre, Sheldon 1980. *Symbolic Interactionism.* Menlo Park, CA: The Benjamin-Cummings Publishing Co.

Taber, Charles 1978. Is There More Than One Way to Do Theology? *Gospel in Context* 1:7-8.

Tippett, Alan 1973. *Verdict Theology in Missionary Theory* (2nd Edition). South Pasadena, CA: William Carey Library.

_____ 1975. Christopaganism or Indigenous Christianity, in *Christo Paganism or Indigenous Christianity,* Tetsunao Yamamori and Charles Taber, eds. South Pasadena, CA: William Carey Library.

Velder, Charles 1963. *"Chao Laung Muak Kham" (The Royal Master with the Gold Crown).* Bangkok: The Journal of the Siam Society: LI: 85-92.

Wrong, Dennis, H. 1961. The Oversocialized Conceptions of Man. *American Sociological Review* 26:183-193.

Index

About The Author

David Filbeck, Ph.D., has served as a missionary of the
Christian Churches/Churches of Christ in Thailand since
1960. He has also taught in Bible college, seminary and
university both in the United States and in Thailand.
Currently he is engaged in evangelism, church planting
and Bible translation in two dialects of Tin, a Mon-
Khmer language located in the northern part of Thailand. In addition to his missionary duties he serves as
Adjunct Professor of Linguistics at William Carey International University, Special Lecturer in Anthropology at
Payap University, Chiang Mai, Thailand, and Lecturer
in Communications at the Haggai Institute, Singapore.